Baby Couture

W9-AAO-584

Samantha McNesby

©2005 Samantha McNesby
Published by

kp books
An Imprint of F+W Publications

700 East State Street • Iola, WI 54990-0001
715-445-2214 • 888-457-2873

Our toll-free number to place an order or obtain a free catalog is (800) 258-0929.

All rights reserved. No portion of this publication may be reproduced or
transmitted in any form or by any means, electronic or mechanical, including
photocopy, recording, or any information storage and retrieval system, without
permission in writing from the publisher, except by a reviewer who may quote
brief passages in a critical article or review to be printed in a magazine or
newspaper, or electronically transmitted on radio, television or the Internet.

Library of Congress Catalog Number: 2004093886

ISBN: 0-87349-774-0

Edited by Candy Wiza
Designed by Emily Adler

Printed in the United States of America

Introduction

Why Baby Couture?

Open any pregnancy or baby magazine today and you will see stylish moms and babies! The mothers-to-be of today are often working professionals, with more disposable income than in the past. They are willing to spend the time and the money to have both a healthy and stylish pregnancy. This desire extends beyond the baby's birth. The same mom who spent a fortune on maternity wear — and, indeed, stylish maternity wear is expensive — wants to maintain the same level of style once the baby arrives.

Top name designers and retailers in the clothing and home furnishing markets have noticed, and many have added stylish baby wear to their lines. Just about every mall in America has a high-end baby boutique. I love to visit and admire (and occasionally buy) the fashions, but the prices can be prohibitive. I really enjoy the "concept" of couture baby wear, but not the price!

As a mom to two babies under the age of 2 (my girls are only 18 months apart) I know how tempting and expensive these new items are. By the time my first baby was 6 months old, I realized I had quite a baby clothing habit! I also took a good, long look at the items my child was wearing, and realized how easy they would be to make. My favorite part of baby and child magazines is the new products: looking at a $30 bib, or a $275 baby blanket, and realizing "I can do that!" I learned that I had a strong preference for high-end baby wear, and that those high-end looks were easy to duplicate at home for a fraction of the cost.

I began researching new trends, and working out simple patterns that would fit my child. I found that babies and toddlers are very easy to fit. Unlike adults or older children, babies have very few "curves," except for their cute chubby tummies. They usually wear garments that have stretchy elastic waists, and most babies are within a few inches of each other height-wise. Once you abandon the traditional view of baby clothing — pink for girls, blue for boys — you will find a huge array of fabrics and design ideas waiting for you. Handcrafted items are durable, safe and made with love. The fact that these projects are stylish as well is an added bonus.

This book is meant to be a source of inspiration, ideas and actual projects for creating your own imaginative and up-to-date fashions for babies and toddlers. The projects in this book are designed with both baby and mom in mind. Each garment is meant to be interesting and useful for baby, with great shapes, textures and colors, but also stylish and fun for mom to sew.

With this book, you will learn to use a few basic patterns to create a variety of looks. Part of the fun of making your own baby wear is the shopping! Browse through the "Getting Started" section to get some ideas, then check out the "Fabric Shopping Guide" for suggestions on selecting and caring for new and vintage fabrics. Learn what projects work best for each stage of baby development, and be sure to visit the safety section as well.

All the projects in the book can be sewn by hand or machine. If you choose to create a project by hand, it will be more time consuming.

Table of Contents

Sewing for babies and toddlers is much easier and a whole lot more fun than sewing for adults. Think about it — the fabrics are more colorful and "fun," the patterns are simple and easy to use, and you can often complete an entire ensemble with a single yard of fabric. The only difficult thing is figuring out where to start.

When I am planning a project, the first thing I do is consider what type of garment I want to make. Do I want a simple dress for a visit to the pumpkin patch, or a more elaborate dress or pant and jacket set for holiday portraits? In some cases, I simply want to make a few cute pairs of pants for playtime, in prints my toddler can choose for herself. Not sure what type of project you want to start with? Check out the "Selecting a Project" and "Selecting a Pattern" sections for more ideas. Once I have decided what I want to make, I either go through my stash of fabrics (which is embarrassingly large) or pay a visit to the fabric store to purchase what I need to complete my project. I like to gather all of my supplies together, from fabrics and patterns to buttons and trims, to be sure I have everything I need before I start. I also thread my sewing machines with matching thread and gather all of my sewing tools.

Once you have everything you need, proceed with your project as directed. Feel free to make modifications to the projects to suit your own individual needs.

Chapter 1 Getting Started

Fabric Shopping Guide

You can find fabrics for your projects in a variety of places. Check out traditional fabric stores, but be sure to look at all of the fabrics, not just the juvenile prints. Fabrics intended for adult clothing and for home décor might just suit your project perfectly!

You also can find fabrics in unusual places — check out antique shops and markets for vintage linens. Single pillowcases are inexpensive, and they are the perfect size for a toddler's dress.

I am always on the lookout for bedspreads and large table linens to use for clothing. Vintage bedspreads provide a great quantity of fabric for a minimal price. The types I prefer to purchase are either vintage, cotton printed spreads, or cotton chenille spreads A full-size chenille bedspread in "craft" condition will yield about four yards of fabric for about $20, or about $5 per yard. New chenille of the same quality is about $25 per yard — a substantial difference in price!

I used a pair of my husband's jeans to make the cowboy bib on page 68, and one of my own corduroy skirts for the appliqué jumper on page 43.

When selecting a fabric, consider the overall quality as well as the print or design. You will waste your time if you make a project that gets worn out after a single washing.

Also, consider the color, print and texture of the fabric. Young babies love bold colors and patterns, and develop an interest in contrasting textures at a very early age. The combination of red, black and white is particularly compelling to young babies.

Follow the directions on page 70 to make a dress from a vintage pillowcase.

Check in your own closet for fabrics to recycle. Adult clothing, especially large skirts, shirts, jeans and jackets are a wonderful source of fabric for baby wear. I always save old wool pieces, as they can be felted and used in a variety of projects.

The bold print and soft, supple flannel make this blanket visually and tactilely attractive to babies.

The fabric you choose should be soft, washable and easy to care for. The projects in this book are not designed for sleepwear. Sleepwear for babies and children always should be made using specially treated fireproof fabrics.

Selecting a Project

Select a project based on your baby's stage of development. Newborns and babies up to 3 months spend most of their time sleeping on their backs, so items with ties or dimensional details at the back would not be comfortable. Babies this age get lots of use from blankets, bibs, hats and simple dresses. My own girls spent most of their first three months in comfy pajamas and onesies, with a hat or blanket as needed. This age group is most interested in bold colors, high contrast patterns and soft, touchable fabric.

Madeline is almost 6 months old and will start crawling very soon.

Babies of 6 months or so start getting a bit more mobile, and often are beginning to eat table food. Bibs for this age group are a must, and these soon-to-be crawlers can wear any of the clothing projects. Most babies in this age range wear the infants or small size.

Babies from 6 months to 1 year old are learning to do so many things! They can sit up, feed themselves, pull to standing, and in some cases, even begin to walk. Most babies in this age group crawl at some point. If your baby is crawling, and you like one of the long dresses, consider making a shorter dress with pants or shorts underneath, like the Rumba shirt on page 88. You still have the look of a dress, but your baby can crawl around in comfort. This mobile age group will prefer smaller bibs, again because of the possibility of stumbling over loose fabric

when crawling or trying to stand. At this age, babies become more diverse in their sizes — our models in this age group were able to wear size small, medium, and in one case, large!

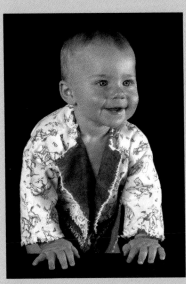

10-month-old Jacob is already learning to stand and walk.

Toddlers 1 year and older are able to walk (though some do this earlier than others) climb, jump, run and play. Clothing for toddlers should fit well, without a lot of extra fabric. Our toddler models range in age from 1 year to 3 years old and wear size medium or large. Your toddler may enjoy helping you pick out a fabric, or have a strong preference for one outfit over another.

A typical active toddler, 18-month-old Sarah just loves to get into things!

Selecting a Pattern

Each of the projects in this book is created using a simple pattern. What makes the projects differ from one another are the fabric choices and the added details. Adding or removing cuffs, pockets, appliqués or bows, or changing the length of a skirt or ruffle can make one outfit look completely different from another, even though they both use the same base pattern.

Another benefit to using the same set of patterns to create a variety of looks is the ease and comfort you develop with the pattern, enabling you to work more efficiently. By the time the photography for this book was finished, I could make a pair of pants, in any size, in under an hour, because I was so accustomed to the pattern and assembly.

Select your project based on what you need. Consider the age and development stage of your baby, your current wardrobe needs, and the time and season of the year.

Choosing a Size

The project sizes in "Baby Couture" are based on measurements. Babies can vary wildly in their height and weight, especially after 6 months of age. It is easier to get a good fit by using measurements.

Use a flexible fabric or plastic tape measure and measure your baby while he or she is in a good mood. Make a game out of it and write down the measurements as you go.

You need both height and weight measurements. For height, it may be easier to have your baby lie down, then measure from head to heel. Toddlers can stand against a wall for a quick measurement.

Note: *If your baby wears cloth diapers, make pants and shorts one size larger than your measurements. Babies wearing cloth diapers have lots of extra fabric on their bottoms and generally need more room in the hip area.*

For weight, use your baby's weight from your most recent pediatrician visit, or step on your home scale holding your baby, then weigh yourself alone. Subtract your weight from the combined weight and the result is the weight of your baby.

Compare your measurements to this chart. If your baby falls between two sizes, in most cases, the larger size will work out better for you. Your baby will have room to grow.

SIZE CHART:

Sizes	INFANTS	SMALL	MEDIUM	LARGE
Height	18"-22"	23"-26"	27"-30"	31"-36"
Weight	6-12 lbs.	13-18 lbs.	19-24 lbs.	25-30 lbs.

Important safety tips for sewing baby clothing:

▶ **While you are sewing, keep all sharp objects away from small children.** Little hands are amazingly fast, and the shiny gleam of scissors, needles and pins seem to have special appeal. I have a sewing basket with a secure closure that slides right under our couch. I put the project I am working on into this box, and put it away any time I take a break. My sewing machines and cutting area are in a completely separate room that is off limits to my children.

▶ **Keep all loose small objects out of reach.** Loose buttons, safety pins, small scraps of fabric and bits of paper are all potential choking hazards. Items that will fit into the opening of a toilet paper roll are a choking hazard for kids under 3. If you are in doubt, put things away when you are through with them.

▶ **Follow the "rule of three" for safety: Sew every button, regardless of its size or placement, three times.** Use a different thread each time, and stitch the button to the fabric at least three times for each thread. So to add a single shank button: Thread your needle with a strong cotton thread. Stitch the button into place, passing several times through the button and fabric. Knot and cut the ends. Repeat two times, for a total of three threads, securing the button to the garment.

▶ **Stitch through dimensional appliqués like yo-yos three times.** Use a different thread each time, and stitch the yo-yo to the fabric at least three times for each thread. To add a yo-yo: Thread your needle with a strong cotton thread. Stitch the yo-yo in place, passing several times through the yo-yo and fabric. Knot and cut the ends. Repeat two times, for a total of three threads, securing the yo-yo to the garment.

▶ **You know your child better than anyone else.** If your baby chews on buttons, then make garments without reachable buttons. You can replace them with another closure for jackets, a decorative detail for other garments, or just omit them entirely. Buttons used in the back of a garment generally are not a concern, as they can't be reached while the garment is worn.

▶ **For tops or dresses with drawstrings, after adding the strings, try the garment on the child.** Tie in place and mark the ties. Remove the garment. Pull the ties to the marked lines and stitch securely in place using matching thread. This will prevent the child from removing the ties; a potential strangulation hazard.

▶ **Do not use loose blankets in the crib or place them on your child for sleeping.** Use blankets as play mats, to cover a child in a carseat carrier, or for decoration only.

▶ **Great care was taken in the selection and presentation of information included in this book, but no warranty is provided, or results guaranteed.** Since we have no control over the procedures used or the choice of materials, neither KP Books nor the author shall have any liability to any person or entity with respect to any loss or damages caused directly or indirectly by the information contained in this book.

Soft muted colors, florals, large and small, tiny gingham checks, fine lace and crochet trims form the backbone of this style. Many shabby and chic-themed baby projects have a traditional, heirloom feel, with lush textures and soft fabrics and finishes. Sweet and pretty, this style is ideal for newborns of both genders and little girls of all ages.

Chapter 2 Shabby & Chic

Rose and Gingham Dress

This dress combines two mini prints, an all-over floral and a simple gingham. I found these fabrics at my local quilt shop. Cottons for quilters are generally top quality, and come in a wide array of colors and patterns. The fabrics used for this dress are coordinates — they were designed to work together and match perfectly. 14-month-old Sarah wears a size medium dress.

Fabrics

1 yd. mini rose print
¾ yd. red gingham
½ yd. ivory lining

Notions

3 ivory ⅜" buttons
Thread to match fabric
Hand or machine sewing needle

Supplies

Patterns from the pattern sheet
  (bodice front and back, sleeves)
Rotary cutter
Ruler
Cutting mat
Scissors
Straight pins
Water-soluble fabric marker
Iron and pressing surface

Cutting Instructions

FROM THE MINI ROSE PRINT, CUT:

Bodice
(1) Bodice front
(2) Bodice backs

Skirt front
Size infants (1) 10" x 18" rectangle
Size small (1) 11" x 20" rectangle
Size medium (1) 13" x 22" rectangle
Size large (1) 14" x 22" rectangle

Skirt backs
Size infants (2) 10" x 8" rectangles
Size small (2) 11" x 9" rectangles
Size medium (2) 13" x 11" rectangles
Size large (2) 14" x 11" rectangles

FROM THE RED GINGHAM, CUT:

Sleeves
(2) Sleeves

Side ties
Size infants or small (2) 3" x 16" strips
Size medium or large (2) 3" x 20" strips

Skirt ruffle
Size infants or small (2) 4" x 36" strips
Size medium or large (2) 5" x 44" strips

FROM THE IVORY LINING, CUT:

Bodice
(1) Bodice front
(2) Bodice backs

Directions

This project uses a ⅝" seam allowance.

1. Make the bodice: Stitch the bodice backs to the bodice front with right sides together at the shoulder seams. Press. Repeat, using the ivory lining fabric.

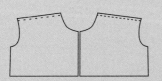

2. Place the ivory bodice piece right-side up on a flat work surface. Top with the print bodice piece; right-side down. Pin at the neck and center back seams, and stitch. Clip the neck seams up to, but not through, the stitching. Turn right-side out and press.

3. Topstitch along the neck and each side of the center back, ¼" from the edge.

4. Add the sleeves: Fold a sleeve piece in half lengthwise with wrong sides together. Stitch along the raw edges. Gather the top of the sleeve between the dots.

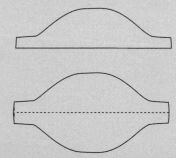

5. Place the bodice with the floral side up. Pin the sleeve in place, matching up the raw edges. Stitch the sleeve. Repeat for the other side. Fold the sleeves into place and press.

6. Fold a side tie in half, right sides together, and stitch the raw edges along the bottom and one side. Turn and press. Repeat for the other side tie.

7. Pin a side tie to each side of the bodice front, 1" from the bottom and matching raw edges. Stitch in place.

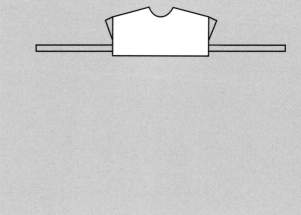

8. Fold the bodice, right sides together, and the side ties facing in. Stitch along each side, from the sleeve to the bottom edge. Turn to the right side and press.

9. With right sides together, stitch the skirt backs to the skirt front. Press.

10. Stitch the short edges of the ruffle strips with right sides together. Press.

11. Fold the ruffle strip in half with wrong sides together. Press. Stitch the raw edges together. Gather the ruffle: Use a brightly-colored thread and gather by hand or machine along the raw edges.

12. Pin the ruffle to the skirt with right sides together. Match up the side edges and adjust the gathering to fit. Stitch in place. Press. Topstitch ¼" from the ruffle.

13. Fold the skirt matching right sides together. Stitch together along the short side, leaving a 5" unstitched portion at one end of the skirt. Press.

14. Gather the skirt: Use a brightly-colored thread and gather by hand or machine along the top 5" unstitched opening edge. Pin the skirt to the bodice with right sides together. Match up the back edges and side seams. Adjust the gathering to fit. Stitch in place. Press.

15. Mark and stitch the buttonholes as shown on the pattern. Mark and stitch the buttons as shown on the pattern.

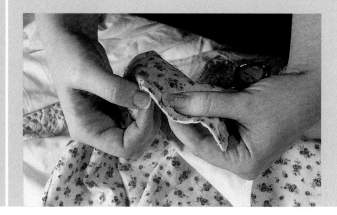

Floral and Gingham Jacket

Don't be afraid to use a large-scale print for children's wear! This rose and bird floral fabric makes a beautiful jacket. When using a mid- to large-size print, choose a pattern that has big pieces, such as a jacket like this one, or a full skirt, to show off the fabric. Check in the home décor section of your local fabric store for a variety of wonderful large prints.

Fabrics
¾ yd. bird and rose print
½ yd. red gingham
¾ yd. ivory lining

Notions
5 red gingham ¾" fabric-covered buttons
  (See page 125 for directions for covering
  the buttons)
Thread to match fabric
Hand or machine sewing needle
Straight pins

Other Supplies
Patterns from the pattern sheet
  (jacket front and back, collar, cuff)
Rotary cutter
Ruler
Cutting mat
Scissors
Water-soluble fabric marker
Iron and pressing surface

Cutting Instructions
FROM THE BIRD AND ROSE PRINT, CUT:

Jacket
(1) Jacket back
(2) Jacket fronts

FROM THE RED GINGHAM, CUT:

Collar and Cuff
(2) Collars
(2) Cuffs

Ruffle
Size infants or small (2) 4" x 24" strips
Size medium or large (2) 5" x 30" strips

FROM THE IVORY LINING, CUT:

Jacket
(1) Jacket back
(2) Jacket fronts

Directions

This project uses a ⅝" seam allowance.

1. With right sides together, stitch the floral jacket fronts to the back at the shoulder seams. Stitch each side seam from the bottom of the jacket to the end of the sleeve. Press. Repeat, using the ivory lining fabric.

2. Place the collar pieces right sides together. Sew all the way around the outer edge. Use scissors to snip the seam allowances every ¼" along the curves. Snip up to, but not over, the stitching. Turn the collar right-side out and press. Topstitch ¼" from the edge. Pin the collar to the neck opening. Stitch in place. Use scissors to snip the seam allowances every ¼" along the curves. Snip up to, but not over, the stitching.

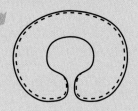

3. Add the ruffle: With right sides together, stitch the short edges of the ruffle strips together. Press. Fold the ruffle strip in half lengthwise, with wrong sides together, and press. Stitch the raw edges together. Gather the ruffle: Use a brightly-colored thread and gather by hand or machine along the raw edges. Pin the ruffle to the floral print jacket bottom with right sides together. Adjust the gathering to fit. Stitch in place. Press.

4. With right sides together, place the floral jacket piece inside the ivory lining piece. Pin in place along the bottom, collar and each side of the front. Stitch the bottom, collar and each side of the front, leaving a 3" opening at the neck back for turning. Use scissors to snip the seam allowances every ¼" along the curves. Snip up to, but not over, the stitching. Turn right-side out and press. Hand stitch the opening closed.

5. Select a gingham cuff piece. Place right sides together, stitch along the short side, and press, forming a ring of fabric. Fold the fabric ring in half, wrong sides together, and press.

6. With the jacket right-side out, insert the cuff into the sleeve opening, lining up the raw edges. Stitch around the edge. Turn the cuff to the right side and press. Use red thread to stitch through the cuffs at each side seam to secure in place. Repeat for the remaining sleeve cuff.

7. Mark and stitch the buttonholes and buttons using the buttonhole guide on the pattern sheet.

Roses Headband

A headband like this one is so fast and easy to make. It's a great accent for just about any outfit. The headband makes a pretty finishing touch for the dress. If your child will not wear a headband, mount the bow on a hair clip instead.

Fabrics

¼ yd. red gingham
⅛ yd. red floral

Notions

1 yd. elastic 1" wide
Thread to match fabric
Hand or machine sewing needle
Straight pins

Other Supplies

Rotary cutter
Ruler
Cutting mat
Water-soluble fabric marker
Scissors
Iron and pressing surface
Safety pin or elastic guide
Tape measure

Cutting Instructions

FROM THE RED GINGHAM, CUT:
(1) 3" square
(1) 3" x 44" strip

FROM THE RED FLORAL, CUT:
(1) 5" x 10" rectangle
(1) 5" x 14" rectangle

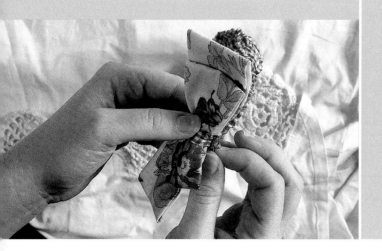

Directions

This project uses a ⅜" seam allowance.

1. Measure your child's head, and add 1". Cut the elastic using this figure as your guide.

2. Make the band: With right sides together, stitch the 3" x 44" red gingham strip along the 44" side. Turn right-side out and press.

3. Attach an elastic guide or safety pin to one end of the elastic. Guide the elastic through the headband tube. Overlap the elastic edges, and stitch securely in place, using several rows of stitching. Adjust the fabric around the headband. Hand stitch the opening closed.

4. Make the bow: With right sides together, stitch the 5" x 10" red floral rectangle along the 10" side. Turn right-side out and press. Fold this piece in half, matching the short sides. Stitch on the short side, forming a ring. Press, moving the seam to the middle of the ring. Repeat, using the 5" x 14" red floral rectangle.

5. With right sides together, stitch the 3" square gingham along one edge. Turn right-side out and press, moving the seam to the middle of the rectangle.

6. Assemble the bow: Stack the floral bow pieces on top of the gingham headband, keeping the seams facing the back. Wrap the center of the stacked bow pieces with thread. Pull the thread tight to gather the fabric at the center. Tie the thread into a knot to secure. Wrap the gingham rectangle around the floral bow piece. Stitch in the back to secure.

I love the soft, washed blues of these fabrics! When you make a bib, select a size based on your baby's age and stage of development. Create a shorter bib for babies who crawl, and a larger bib for older babies who are learning to feed themselves.

Fabrics
1 fat quarter large blue floral
1 fat quarter ivory or white chenille
1 fat eighth small blue floral

Notions
12" flat ¾" lace
1 white ¾" hook and loop tape dot
Thread to match fabric
Hand or machine needle
Straight pins

Other Supplies
Pattern from the pattern sheet (bib)
Rotary cutter
Cutting mat   Ruler
Clear plastic template sheet   Scissors
Water-soluble fabric marker   Pencil
Iron and pressing surface   Fabric glue

Cutting Instructions
FROM THE LARGE FLORAL, CUT:
(1) 10" square

FROM THE SMALL FLORAL, CUT:
(1) 5" x 10" rectangle

FROM THE CHENILLE, CUT:
(1) 15" square

Directions
This project uses a ⅜" seam allowance.

1. Make a plastic template for the bib pattern: Use a pencil to trace the bib pattern onto the clear plastic template sheet. Cut out the bib template.

2. Make the bib front: With right sides together, stitch the 5" x 10" small floral rectangle to the large floral 10" square. Press. Stitch the lace on the front of the bib, covering the seam.

3. Cut two bibs: Place the bib front fabric, right-side up, on a flat work surface. Place the bib pattern template on top of the fabric. Move the pattern around until you are happy with the way it will look. (Experiment with different areas of the fabric until you find the one you like.) Trace around the bib pattern with a water-soluble fabric marker. Repeat, using the chenille fabric for the bib back.

4. Place the bib pieces right sides together. Sew all the way around the bib, leaving a 3" opening for turning. Use scissors to snip the seam allowances every ¼" along the curves. Snip up to, but not over, the stitching. Turn the bib right-side out and press. Hand stitch the opening closed.

5. Use fabric glue to attach the hook and loop tape dot to the neck portion of the bib. Let the glue dry for 48 hours before washing or wearing.
Note: *The neck edges overlap when the bib is worn.*

Vintage Fabric Shorts

The fabric used for this project came from an old floral bedspread. The spread was quilted, but very lightweight. As a simple finishing touch, I added a touch of pretty crocheted lace to the leg openings. Using lace also eliminates the need for a hem.

Fabric

36" square vintage or new floral quilted fabric

Notions

1 yd. white 1" crocheted lace
1" wide elastic for the following:
    Size small 17"
    Size medium 18½"
    Size large 20"
Thread to match fabric
Hand or machine sewing needle
Straight pins

Other Supplies

Pattern from the pattern sheet (shorts)
Scissors
Iron and pressing surface
Safety pin or elastic guide

Cutting Instructions

FROM THE QUILTED FLORAL, CUT:
(4) Shorts
Note: *With right sides together, fold the vintage/new fabric in half. Pin the shorts pattern to the fabric and cut out.*

FROM THE CROCHETED LACE, CUT:
(2) 18" pieces

Directions

This project uses a ⅝" seam allowance.

1. Place one shorts piece right-side up on a flat work surface. Top with a second piece, right-side down. Pin together along the long straight side and stitch. Press open. Repeat, using the remaining shorts pieces.

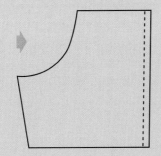

2. Add the lace: Place one stitched shorts piece right-side up on a flat work surface. Place the lace on top of the shorts, with the decorative edge of the lace facing the right side of the shorts. Stitch in place. Press the seam. Topstitch ¼" from the edge. Repeat, using the second shorts piece and the remaining lace.

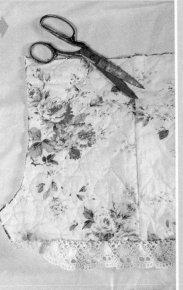

3. Fold a shorts piece with right sides together. Pin along the short straight side and stitch. Press. Repeat, using the remaining shorts piece.

4. Assemble the shorts: With right sides together, place one shorts piece inside the other. Stitch along the curved center seam. Turn the shorts right-side out and press.

5. Turn the shorts inside out. Finish the top edge of the shorts using a serger, or fold under ¼", and stitch in place.

6. Fold the top edge of the shorts down 1½". Stitch in place, leaving a 3" opening to insert the elastic.

7. Attach an elastic guide or safety pin to one end of the elastic. Guide the elastic through the waistband. Overlap the edges, and stitch securely in place, using several rows of stitching. Adjust the fabric around the waistband and check the fit. Stitch the opening closed.

Sweet Scrappy Baby Quilt

Pretty scraps of pastel fabrics make a snuggly cover for your favorite baby. This quilt is fast and easy to make. All the pieces are the same size. A project both you and your baby will enjoy.

Fabrics

3 yd. assorted scraps of solids and prints in the following colors: light pink, medium pink, ivory, pale green, butter yellow (At least half of the fabrics should be pinks.)
1½ yd. ivory flannel

Notions

9½ yd. ivory 2" satin baby blanket binding
Thread to match fabric
Hand or machine sewing needle
Straight pins
Crib-size quilt batting (45" x 60")

Other Supplies

Rotary cutter
Ruler
Cutting mat
Water-soluble fabric marker
Scissors
Iron and pressing surface

Cutting Instructions

FROM THE SOLIDS AND PRINTS, CUT:
(60) 5" squares of assorted pink fabrics
(60) 5" squares of remaining assorted fabrics

FROM THE IVORY FLANNEL, CUT:
(1) 44" x 48" rectangle

FROM THE BATTING, CUT:
(1) 44" x 48" rectangle

Note: *Use a rotary cutter, ruler and cutting mat to cut your fabrics. Try stacking your cotton fabrics to cut as many as 10 at a time.*

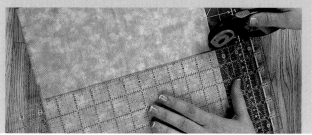

Directions

Finished size: 46"x 50" with binding.
This project uses a ½" seam allowance.

1. Lay your quilt out on a large, flat surface — a large dining room table or the floor works best. Alternate the pink squares with other assorted colors, and move the pieces around until you are happy with the look.

2. When you are happy with the layout, begin piecing. Start with the top row and sew the pieces together in order. Keep right sides together. Once the row is sewn, place it back on your layout surface so you can keep the pieces in order. Repeat for each row.

3. Once you have sewn all of the individual squares into rows, stitch the rows together.

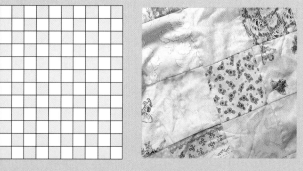

4. Place the flannel on a flat work surface with the right-side down. Top with batting, then the quilt top, with the right-side up. Baste and quilt as desired. The sample is machine quilted "in the ditch," or along each seam.

5. Follow the manufacturer's directions to add the blanket binding to the quilt edges.

Orient style is a trend that has been emerging for quite a while. Mainstream stores like the Gap® and Target® both have Asian-themed baby items in their recent advertising. The bold black-white-red combinations of Orient Style are the first colors a baby can see well — many early development toys feature black, white and red color combinations. "Hello Kitty"® and other Sanrio® icons are almost as popular in the United States as they are overseas, and soft baby kimono and pajama sets are being sold in upscale catalogs and boutiques. This style works well for both boys and girls of all ages.

Chapter 3 Orient Style

Blue Newsprint Jacket

This project begins with a pre-made sweatshirt. The great thing about starting with a ready-made item is that someone else has already done some of the work for you! Select a sweatshirt one size larger than your baby currently wears. Wash and dry it before beginning the project. Select your print fabrics first, then choose a sweatshirt to match.

Fabrics (for all sizes)

¼ yd. navy blue Asian newsprint
¼ yd. red marble-print

Notions

Hand or machine sewing needle
Navy and red sewing thread
Straight pins
2 buttons ¾" or 1"

Other Supplies

Navy sweatshirt
Scissors
Ruler
Water-soluble fabric marker or chalk pencil
Iron and pressing surface

Cutting Instructions

FROM THE NAVY NEWSPRINT, CUT:
(2) 4½" squares (pocket front)
(2) 4½" x 5½" rectangles (lining)
(1) 2½" x 30" strip

FROM THE RED MARBLED PRINT, CUT:
(2) 4½" x 1½" rectangles

Directions

The seam allowance for this project is ⅜" unless otherwise stated.

1. Place the sweatshirt on a flat work surface and press. Use scissors to cut off the ribbed cuffs at the sleeves and at the bottom of the shirt.

2. Use the ruler and water-soluble marker to find and mark the center front of the sweatshirt. Cut along the center front.

3. Add the cuffs: Use a rotary cutter, mat and ruler, or a ruler and scissors to cut two rectangles from the newsprint fabric. Each rectangle should be 2½" wide. To determine the length of the rectangle, measure across the sleeve opening. Multiply this measurement by 2, then add ½".
For example, if the sweatshirt sleeve opening is 3": (3" x 2 = 6") and (6" + ½" = 6½"). As a result, the rectangles for this shirt are 6½" x 2½".

4. Select one cuff piece. Place right sides together, stitch along the short side, and press, forming a ring of fabric. Fold the fabric ring in half with wrong sides together. Match up the raw edges and press. Repeat, for the remaining cuff.

5. Place the sweatshirt right-side out and insert the cuff into the sleeve, lining up the raw edges. Stitch around the edge. Turn the cuff to the outside and press in place. Use red thread to stitch through the cuff at each side seam to secure in place. Repeat for the other sleeve.

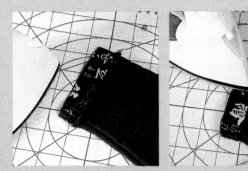

6. Add the binding: With right sides together, and using a 1" seam allowance, stitch the 2½" x 30" newsprint strip along the bottom edge of the jacket. You will have some fabric left over at the end. Trim away any excess newsprint fabric. Press. Finish the raw edge with a serger, or turn under ¼" and stitch in place.

7. Place the jacket on a flat work surface. Press the newsprint fabric under, leaving a 1" strip around the bottom edge of the jacket. Hand stitch in place.

8. Make the pockets: With right sides together, stitch a 4½" x 1½" red rectangle to a 4½" newsprint square. Press.

9. Place a pocket piece and lining piece, right sides together, and sew all the way around, leaving a 2" opening for turning. Turn the pocket right-side out and press. Hand stitch the opening closed. Repeat for the second pocket.

10. Hand stitch the pockets in place on the front of the jacket, 1" from the side seams and bottom binding. Securely hand stitch a button to the center front of each pocket. See page 11 for important safety instructions for adding buttons to children's clothing.

11. Fold the front opening raw edges under ½" and pin in place. Press. Hand or machine stitch to secure.

This fast and easy-to-make outfit works for both infants and toddlers. 8-month-old Drake is wearing a size small newsprint jacket and pants.

Asian Newsprint Pants

Fabric (for all sizes)
¾ yd. navy blue Asian newsprint

Notions
¾" wide elastic for the following:
    Size small 17"
    Size medium 18¼"
    Size large 20"
Thread to match fabric
Hand or machine sewing needle
Straight pins

Other Supplies
Pattern from the pattern sheet (pants)
Scissors
Safety pin or elastic guide
Iron and pressing surface

Cutting Instructions
FROM THE NAVY NEWSPRINT, CUT:
(4) Pants (2 fronts and 2 backs)
Note: This fabric is directional, so be sure to cut all of the pants with the text facing in the same, upright direction.

Wear these pants with or without the coordinating jacket for a sleek, updated look. The pants are hemmed, but you can always add cuffs to the bottom if you prefer them. Use coordinating fabrics and follow the directions on page 42 for adding the cuffs.

Directions

This project uses a ⅝" seam allowance.

1. With right sides together, stitch a pants front to a back at side seams. Stitch the front to the back at the inner leg seams. Press. Repeat for the second front and back.

2. With right sides together, insert one pants leg inside the other. Pin the curved center seam and stitch. If you are not using a serger, finish this seam as desired. Press.

3. Turn the pants inside out. Finish the top opening of the pants using a serger, or fold under ¼", and stitch in place.

4. Place the pants, inside out, on a flat pressing surface. Turn the top of the pants down 1¼" to form a casing for the elastic. Press.

5. Stitch the casing: Stitch around the top of the pants at the lower edge of the casing, leaving a 2" opening for inserting the elastic. Add a second row of stitches ¼" above the first, leaving a 2" opening for inserting the elastic. Stitch around the top of the pants, ⅛" from the folded edge.

6. Attach an elastic guide or safety pin to one end of the elastic. Guide the elastic through the waistband. Overlap the edges, and stitch securely in place, using several rows of stitching. Adjust the fabric evenly around the waistband and check the fit. Stitch the opening closed.

7. Finish the leg openings of the pants using a serger, or fold under ¼" and stitch in place. Fold under 1", and hand stitch in place.

Kitty Cat Jacket

This project begins with a ready-made sweatshirt. Most craft shops carry a selection of plain sweatshirts for children. Choose a sweatshirt one size larger than your baby currently wears, and wash and dry it before beginning. The cat fabric shown here is somewhat "girlish." Choose a more masculine print when making this outfit for a boy.

Fabrics (for all sizes)

1 fat quarter white-black-red kitty print
¼ yd. red marbled solid
1 fat quarter white solid (pocket lining and
   back appliqué)

Notions

2 black ⅝" fabric-covered buttons
   (The sample uses black fabric-covered buttons
   made using black fabric and a covered buttons
   kit. See directions for fabric-covered buttons on
   page 125.)
Hand or machine sewing needle
Black sewing thread
Straight pins

Other Supplies

Black sweatshirt
Plastic template sheet
8" round dinner plate (9" for size large)
Scissors
Ruler
Water-soluble fabric marker or chalk pencil
Iron and pressing surface

Cutting Instructions

FROM THE RED MARBLED SOLID, CUT:
(1) 2½" x 30" binding strip
(2) 4½" x 1½" rectangles

FROM THE KITTY PRINT, CUT:
(2) 4½" squares

FROM THE WHITE SOLID, CUT:
(2) 4½" x 5½" rectangles

Directions

This project uses a ⅜" seam allowance unless
otherwise noted.

1. Place the sweatshirt on a flat work surface and
press. Use scissors to cut off the ribbed cuffs at the
sleeves and at the bottom of the shirt.

2. Use the ruler and water-soluble marker to find and
mark the center front of the sweatshirt. Cut along the
center front.

3. Add the cuffs: Use a rotary cutter, mat and ruler,
or a ruler and scissors to cut two rectangles from the
red fabric. Each rectangle should be 2½" wide. To
determine the length of the rectangle, measure across
the sleeve opening. Multiply this measurement by 2,
and then add ½".
*For example, if the sweatshirt sleeve opening is 3":
(3" x 2 = 6") and (6" + ½" = 6½"). As a result, the
rectangles for this shirt are 6½" x 2½"*

4. Select one cuff piece. Place right sides together,
stitch along the short side, and press, forming a ring
of fabric. Fold the fabric ring in half, wrong sides
together, and press. Repeat for the other cuff.

5. With the sweatshirt right-side out, insert the cuffs into the sleeves, lining up the raw edges. Stitch around the edge. Turn the cuffs right-side out and press in place. Use red thread to stitch through the cuffs at each side seam to secure in place.

6. Add the binding: With right sides together, and using a 1" seam allowance, stitch the 2½" x 30" red marbled binding strip along the bottom edge of the jacket. You will have some fabric left over at the end. Trim away any excess red fabric. Press.

7. Place the jacket on a flat work surface. Press the red fabric under, leaving a 1" strip around the bottom edge of the jacket. Hand stitch in place.

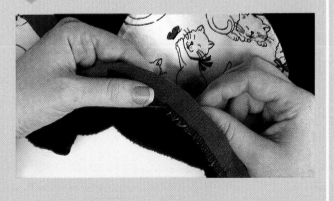

8. Make the pockets: With the right sides together, stitch a 4½" x 1½" red solid rectangle to a 4½" square kitty cat print. Press.

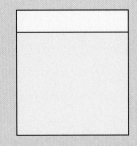

9. Place the red-kitty and white pocket pieces right sides together. Sew all the way around, leaving a 2" opening for turning. Turn the pocket right-side out and press. Hand stitch the opening closed. Repeat for the second pocket.

10. Hand stitch the pockets in place on the front of the jacket, 1" from the side seams and bottom binding. Securely hand stitch a button to the center front of each pocket. See page 11 for important safety instructions for adding buttons to children's clothing.

11. Make the appliqué: Place the plate, face down, on the plastic template sheet. Use a pencil to trace around the edges of the plate. Cut out the template.

12. Place the kitty cat fabric right-side up on a flat work surface. Place the circle template on top of the fabric. Move the template around until you are happy with the way it will look. (Experiment with different areas of the fabric until you find the one you like.) Trace around the circle template with a water-soluble fabric marker. Cut out the circle. Repeat, using the white lining fabric.

13. Place the circles right sides together. Sew all the way around, leaving a 2" opening for turning. Turn the circles right-side out and press. Hand stitch the opening closed. Hand stitch the appliqué in place on the back of the jacket, centering carefully.

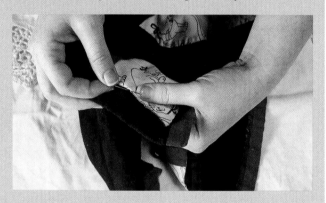

14. Fold the jacket front opening raw edges under ½" and pin in place. Press. Hand or machine stitch to secure.

Sarah is 18 months old and wears a size medium. This set is perfect for outdoor playtime in the spring or fall.

Cat Pants

Fabrics (for all sizes)
⅝ yd. white-black-red cat print
⅛ yd. black on black print

Notions
16" black ⅜" grosgrain ribbon
⅝" wide elastic for the following:
   Size small 17"
   Size medium 18½"
   Size large 20"
Thread to match fabric
Hand or machine sewing needle
Straight pins

Other Supplies
Patterns from the pattern sheet
 (pants front and back, cuffs)
Scissors
Iron and pressing surface
Safety pin or elastic guide

Cutting Instructions
FROM THE CAT PRINT, CUT:
(4) Pants (2 fronts and 2 backs)
Note: *This fabric is directional, so be sure to cut all of the pants with the cats facing in the same, upright direction.*

FROM THE BLACK PRINT, CUT:
(2) Cuffs

Once I realized how easy it was to make pants for my daughter, I never purchased a ready-made pair again! Give yourself about an hour to make these clean and simple pants. This is a perfect project to work on while your baby naps.

Directions

This project uses a ⅝" seam allowance.

1. With the right sides together, stitch a pants front to a back at side seams. Stitch the front to the back at the inner leg seams. Press. Repeat for the second front and back.

2. With the right sides together, insert one pants leg inside of the other. Pin the curved center seam, and stitch. If you are not using a serger, finish this seam as desired. Press.

3. Turn the pants inside out. Finish the top edge of the pants using a serger, or fold under ¼", and stitch in place.

4. Place the pants, inside out, on a flat pressing surface. Turn the top of the pants down 1¼" to form a casing for the elastic. Press.

5. Stitch the casing: Stitch around the top of the pants at the lower edge of the casing, leaving a 2" opening for inserting the elastic. Add a second row of stitches ¼" above the first, leaving a 2" opening for inserting the elastic. Stitch around the top of the pants, ⅛" from the folded edge.

6. Attach an elastic guide or safety pin to one end of the elastic. Guide the elastic through the waistband. Overlap the edges, and stitch securely in place, using several rows of stitching. Adjust the fabric evenly around the waistband and check the fit. Stitch the opening closed.

7. Add the cuffs: Select one cuff piece. Place right sides together. Stitch along the short side and press, forming a ring of fabric. Fold the fabric ring in half with wrong sides together. Press.

8. With the pants right-side out, insert the cuff into the pants leg, lining up the raw edges. Stitch around the edge. Turn the cuff to the outside and press in place. Use black thread to stitch through the cuffs at each side seam to secure in place.

9. Fold the grosgrain ribbon in half to find the center. Securely stitch the ribbon in place through all layers at the center front of the pants. See safety information on page 11 for tips on attaching embellishments to children's clothing. Tie into a bow.

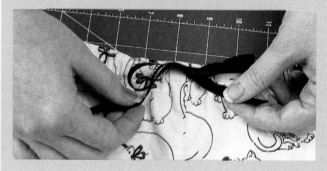

Patchwork Jumper

This project uses a simple, finished-edge appliqué technique with no fusing or tricky needlework required. I chose to use wide-wale corduroy for the jumper, but you could substitute heavy flannel or wool as needed. Add a long sleeve shirt and tights to complete the ensemble.

Fabrics

1 yd. dark green wide-wale corduroy
½ yd. black or dark green cotton (facings)
1 fat quarter multicolored Asian cotton print

Notions

2 red gingham ⅝" fabric-covered buttons (See
   page 125 for directions for covering buttons)
Thread to match fabric
Hand or machine sewing needle
Straight pins

Other Supplies

Patterns from the pattern sheet
   (jumper front and back and
   front and back facings)
Rotary cutter
Ruler
Mat
Water-soluble fabric marker
Scissors
Iron and pressing surface

Cutting Instructions

FROM THE GREEN CORDUROY, CUT:
(1) Jumper/sundress front
(1) Jumper/sundress back

FROM THE BLACK or GREEN COTTON, CUT:
(1) Front facing
(1) Back facing

FROM THE MULTICOLORED ASIAN PRINT, CUT:
(2) 5½" squares
(10) 2" squares

Directions

This project uses a ⅝" seam allowance.

1. Make the appliqués: Place the 5½" square appliqué pieces right sides together. Sew all the way around the appliqué, leaving a 2" opening for turning. Use scissors to snip the seam allowances every ¼". Snip up to, but not over, the stitching. Turn the square right-side out and press. Hand stitch the opening closed.

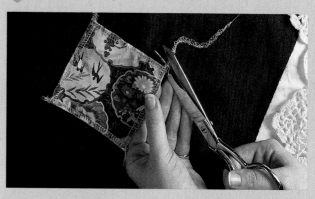

2. Place two 2" square appliqué pieces right sides together. Sew all the way around the appliqué, leaving a small opening for turning. Use scissors to snip the seam allowances every ¼". Snip up to, but not over, the stitching. Turn the square right-side out and press. Hand stitch the opening closed. Repeat for the remaining squares.

3. Place the jumper front right-side up on a flat work surface. Top with the front facing, with the right-side down. Pin at the neck, shoulders and armholes. Stitch in place. Clip the seams up to, but not through, the stitching. Turn right-side out and press. Repeat, attaching the back facing to the jumper back.

4. Topstitch along the neck, armholes and shoulders of each piece, ¼" from the edge.

5. Add the appliqués: Place the jumper front right-side up on a flat work surface. Top with the 5" square appliqué. Center the appliqué on the front of the jumper and pin in place. Stitch to secure.
Note: White thread is for demonstration purposes only. Use matching thread to complete the garment.

6. Place the jumper front right-side up on a flat work surface. Top with the 2" square appliqués. Center the appliqués along the bottom front of the jumper, about 2" from the edge, and pin in place. Stitch to secure.

7. With right sides together, stitch the jumper front to the back along the sides. Turn right-side out and press.

8. Finish the hem of the jumper using a serger, or zigzag stitch along the edge. Fold under ¼" and stitch in place.

9. Mark and stitch the buttonholes as shown on the pattern. Mark and securely hand stitch the buttons. See page 11 for important safety instructions for adding buttons to children's clothing.

Note: Since jumpers are usually worn with a shirt underneath, you might want to go up a size when making this project to ensure a proper fit.

3-year-old Ally is wearing a size large jumper.

Asian Text Blanket

This is one of my favorite and most versatile projects! Whenever I use this blanket, I get tons of people asking me where I bought it. Your baby will love the vivid colors and varied textures of the striking yet simple project.

Fabrics

1 yd. black-red Asian-style text print
1 yd. bright red flannel

Notions

1 yd. lightweight fusible web
 (at least 36" wide)
2 packages black pre-made ½" seam binding
Hand or machine sewing needle
Black sewing thread
Straight pins

Other Supplies

Rotary cutter
Ruler
Cutting mat
9" plate or dish
Water-soluble fabric marker
Scissors
Iron and pressing surface

Cutting Instructions

FROM THE BLACK-RED PRINT, CUT:
(1) 36" square

FROM THE RED FLANNEL, CUT:
(1) 36" square

FROM THE FUSIBLE WEB, CUT:
(1) 36" square

Directions

1. This project uses a ¼" seam allowance. Fuse the fabrics: Lay the red flannel fabric right-side down on your work surface. Top with the fusible web, paper side up. Follow the manufacturer's directions to fuse in place. Let cool, then peel off the paper.

2. Lay the red flannel square right-side down. Place the red-black print on top, right-side up. Line up the raw edges and press.

3. Shape the corners: Lay the blanket on a flat work surface. Place a 9" dinner plate on one corner of the blanket, lining up the edges of the plate with the corner edges of the blanket. The corner of the fabric will extend beyond the plate. Use a water-soluble fabric marker to trace around the edge of the plate.

4. Use scissors to cut along the traced line along the corner. Repeat for the remaining three corners.

5. Assemble the binding: Open the packages of binding. Unfold and press lightly to remove any creases from the binding. Open out one end of the strip of binding and press. Repeat for the second strip of binding. With right sides together, stitch the two binding strips together along the open short side. Refold this section and press.

6. Follow the manufacturer's directions to attach the binding.

Sushi Cats Bib

When I saw this adorable fabric at a quilt show last year, I just had to have it. I didn't have a project in mind, but it was too neat to pass up! An interesting fabric like this one needs only a simple design to show it off. This bib has only two pieces, so you'll be able to complete it in about an hour.

Fabrics

1 fat quarter sushi cats or other novelty print
1 fat quarter black cotton or flannel

Notions

1 black ¾" wide hook and loop tape dot
Hand or machine sewing needle
Black sewing thread
Straight pins

Other Supplies

Pattern from the pattern sheet (bib)
Clear plastic template sheet
Pencil
Water-soluble fabric marker
Scissors
Fabric glue
Iron and pressing surface

Directions

This project uses a ¼" seam allowance.

1. Make a plastic template: Use a pencil to trace the bib pattern onto the clear plastic template sheet. Cut out the bib template.

2. Cut two bibs: Place the sushi cats print right-side up on a flat work surface. Place the plastic bib template on top of the fabric. Move the template around until you are happy with the way it will look. (Experiment with different areas of the fabric until you find the one you like.) Trace around the bib template with a water-soluble fabric marker. Repeat, using the black fabric for the bib back. ⬇

3. Place the bib pieces right sides together. Sew all the way around the bib, leaving a 3" opening for turning. Use scissors to snip the seam allowances every ¼" along the curves. Snip up to, but not over, the stitching. Turn the bib right-side out and press. Hand stitch the opening closed. ⬇

4. Use fabric glue to attach the hook and loop tape dot to the neck portion of the bib. Let the glue dry for 48 hours before washing or wearing.
Note: *The neck edges overlap when the bib is worn.*

⬅

Reversible Hat

Hats are a quick and versatile addition to your baby's wardrobe. This one is reversible, which means you get twice the use and looks from a single project. Don't be surprised at the size of the pattern pieces — babies and toddlers have large heads!

Fabrics

½ yd. red-black Asian newsprint fabric
½ yd. black cotton or flannel

Notions

½ yd. lightweight fusible interfacing
Thread to match fabric
Hand or machine sewing needle
Straight pins

Other Supplies

Patterns from the pattern sheet
  (hat top, hat side, brim)
Scissors
Iron and pressing surface

Cutting Instructions

Note: *Follow the manufacturer's instructions to attach the fusible interfacing to the wrong side of the black fabric. (The interfacing will give the hat more body and help it keep its shape.)*

FROM THE RED-BLACK NEWSPRINT, CUT:
(1) Hat top
(1) Hat side
(1) Hat brim

FROM THE FUSED BLACK COTTON, CUT:
(1) Hat top
(1) Hat side
(1) Hat brim

Directions

This project uses a ⅝" seam allowance.

1. With right sides together, stitch the short ends of the red hat sides together, forming a ring of fabric. Turn right-side out and press. Repeat, using the black hat sides. With right sides together, stitch the short ends of the red hat brim together, forming a ring of fabric. Turn right-side out and press. Repeat, using the black hat brim.

2. Gather the red hat top: Use a brightly-colored thread and gather by hand or machine along the raw edges. With right sides together, pin the red hat side to the top. Match up the raw edges and adjust the gathering to fit. Stitch in place. Press.

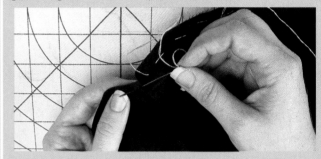

3. With right sides together, pin the red hat brim to the hat side. Match up the raw edges and stitch in place. Press. Repeat to assemble the black side of the hat.

4. Place the assembled hat pieces with right sides together. Sew all the way around the brim, leaving a 3" opening for turning. Use scissors to snip the seam allowances every ¼" along the curves. Snip up to, but not over, the stitching. Turn the hat right-side out and press. Hand stitch the opening closed.

5. Top stitch the hat brim, ¼" from the edge, using black thread.

Wear this reversible hat as a red hat with a black rim, or a black hat with a red rim. Your baby will likely choose a favorite side! Jacob, almost 10 months old, is wearing a size medium hat.

The 1930s reproduction prints, which are so popular with quilters, are driving a great trend for babies. Retailers and designers have discovered the not-too-sweet colors and fabrics, paired with vintage images, are a sure hit with consumers of all ages — and babies are no exception. Nostalgia projects are charming, homey and reminiscent of a simpler era. Flour sack prints, tea-dyed homespun cotton, soft laundered denim and chenille are hallmarks of nostalgia style. The medium toned pinks, blues, greens and yellows of nostalgia style make it ideal for girls or boys — this is a great choice when the baby's gender will be a surprise!

Chapter 4 Nostalgia

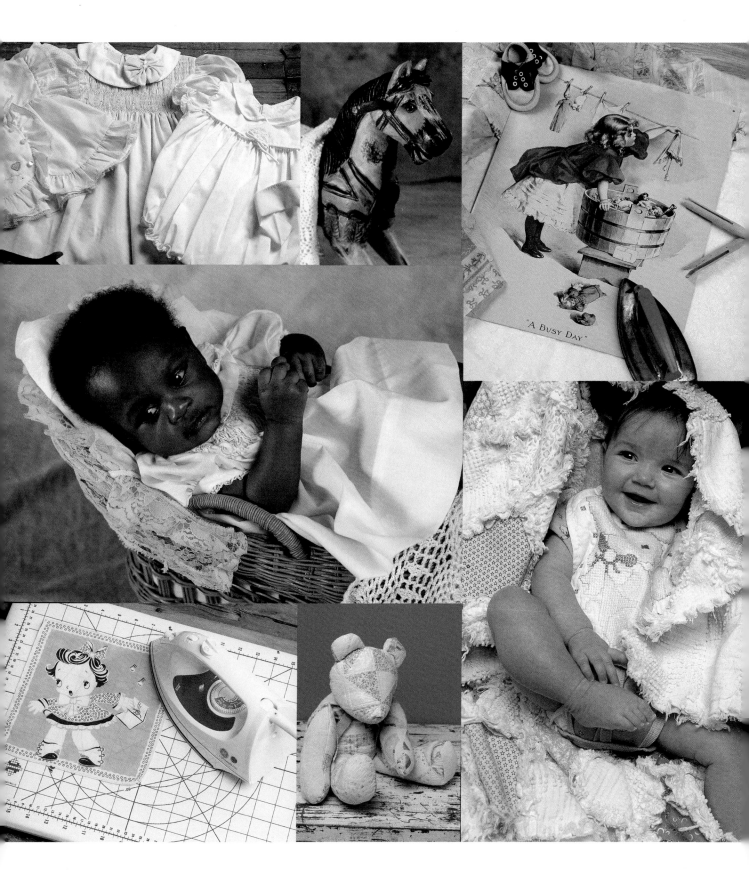

Polka Dot and Gingham Jacket

I had a difficult time deciding which fabric should be the outside of this jacket and which should be the lining. After much deliberation, I chose the polka dot for its bright ground and retro feel. If you prefer, complete this project with the gingham side out.

Fabrics
¾ yd. green-white polka dot
¾ yd. green-white gingham
½ yd. white chenille

Notions
7 white ¾" buttons
White sewing thread
Hand or machine sewing needle
Straight pins

Other Supplies
Patterns from the pattern sheet
  (jacket front and back, collar, cuff)
Rotary cutter
Ruler
Cutting mat
Scissors
Water-soluble fabric marker
Iron and pressing surface

Cutting Instructions
FROM THE POLKA DOT, CUT:
(1) Jacket back
(2) Jacket fronts
(1) Collar
(2) 4½" x 5½" rectangles (pocket lining)

FROM THE CHENILLE, CUT:
(1) Collar
(2) Cuffs
(2) 4½" x 1½" rectangles (pocket trim)

FROM THE GINGHAM, CUT:
(1) Jacket back
(2) Jacket fronts
(2) 4½" squares (pockets)

Directions
This project uses a ⅝" seam allowance.

1. With the right sides together, stitch the polka dot jacket fronts to the back at the shoulder seams. Stitch each side seam from the bottom of the jacket to the end of the sleeve. Press. Repeat, using the gingham fabric.

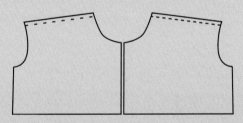

2. Place the collar pieces right sides together. Sew all the way around the outer edge. Use scissors to snip the seam allowances every ¼" along the curves. Snip up to, but not over, the stitching. Turn the collar right-side out and press. Topstitch ¼" from the edge.

3. Pin the collar to the neck opening, matching right sides of the chenille and gingham. Stitch in place. Use scissors to snip the seam allowances every ¼" along the curves. Snip up to, but not over, the stitching.

4. With right sides together, stitch a 4½" x 1½" chenille rectangle to a 4½" gingham pocket square. Press.

5. Place the chenille/gingham and polka dot pocket pieces with right sides together. Sew all the way around the pocket, leaving a 2" opening for turning. Turn the pocket right-side out and press. Hand stitch the opening closed. Repeat for the second pocket.

6. Hand stitch the pockets in place on the front of the jacket, 2" from the side seams and bottom edge. Securely hand stitch a button to the center front of each pocket. See page 11 for important safety instructions for adding buttons to children's clothing.

7. With right sides together, place the polka dot jacket piece inside of the gingham lining piece. Pin in place along the bottom, neckline and each side of the front. Stitch the bottom, collar and each side of the front, leaving a 3" opening at the back neck for turning. Use scissors to snip the seam allowances every ¼" along the curves. Snip up to, but not over, the stitching. Turn right-side out and press. Hand stitch the opening closed.

8. Select a chenille cuff piece. Place right sides together, stitch along the short side, and press, forming a ring of fabric. Fold the fabric ring in half with the wrong sides together. Press.

9. With the jacket right-side out, insert the cuff into the sleeve opening, lining up the raw edges. Stitch around the edge. Turn the cuff to the outside and press in place. Use white thread to stitch through the cuff at each side seam to secure in place. Repeat for the remaining sleeve cuff.

10. Mark and stitch the buttonholes and buttons using the buttonhole guide from the pattern insert. See page 11 for important safety instructions for adding buttons to children's clothing.

Cowboy Jacket

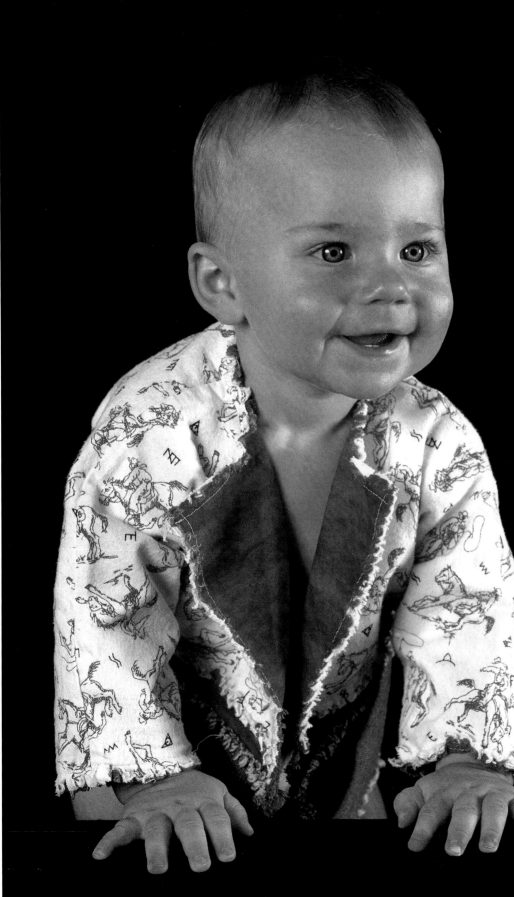

The raw edges of this jacket are left exposed, creating a soft fringed effect. Leaving the edges unfinished also means that this jacket can be completed very quickly. It is a great project for beginners. Make this cute piece of clothing in just a single sewing session. Replace the cowboy print with a flowery flannel to make this jacket for a little girl.

Fabrics

1 yd. vintage cowboy or other novelty print
½ yd. recycled or new denim
1 yd. red flannel

Notions

Thread to match fabric
Hand or machine sewing needle
Straight pins

Other Supplies

Pattern from the pattern sheet
  (jacket front and back)
Rotary cutter
Ruler
Cutting mat
Fabric marker
Water-soluble fabric marker
Scissors
Iron and pressing surface

Cutting Instructions

FROM THE VINTAGE COWBOY PRINT, CUT:
(2) 20" squares
(1) 40" x 20" rectangle

FROM THE RED FLANNEL, CUT:
(2) 1" x 20" strips
(1) 1" x 40" strip
(1) Jacket back
(2) Jacket fronts

FROM THE DENIM, CUT:
(2) 5" x 20" strips
(1) 5" x 40" strip

Directions

This project uses a ⅝" seam allowance.

1. Piece the jacket front and back.
Back:
With the wrong sides together, stitch the 1" x 40" red flannel strip to the 40" x 20" cowboy print along the 40" edge.

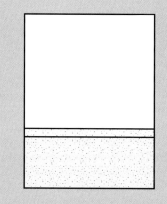

2. With the wrong sides together, stitch the 5" x 40" denim strip to the red flannel piece along the 40" edge.

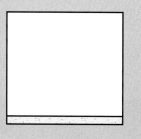

Front:

3. With wrong sides together, stitch a 1" x 20" red flannel strip to the 20" square of cowboy print. With wrong sides together, stitch a 5" x 20" denim strip to the red flannel along the 20" edge. Repeat for the remaining front fabric piece.

4. Cut the pieced fabrics:

FROM THE COWBOY COMBO FABRICS, CUT:
(1) Jacket back
(2) Jacket fronts

5. With right sides together, stitch the cowboy jacket fronts to the back at the shoulder seams. Stitch each side seam from the bottom of the jacket to the end of the sleeve. Press. Repeat, using the red lining pieces.

6. With the wrong sides together, place the red lining piece inside of the cowboy jacket piece. Pin in place along the bottom, neckline and each side of the front.

7. Stitch the bottom, neckline, sleeve openings and each side of the front. Use scissors to snip the seam allowances every ¼". Snip up to, but not over, the stitching. Wash and dry the jacket.

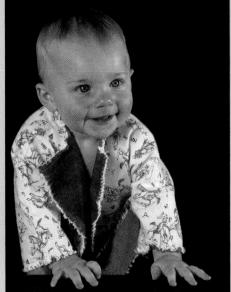

Jacob is wearing a size medium jacket.

Denim Striped Pants

This denim has a lovely vintage-style ticking pattern. Be sure to wash and dry new denim before using, or it may shrink considerably, altering the look or fit of your project. I paired the striped denim with red for a great, vintage boys look. The finished pants remind me of an old-fashioned baseball uniform.

Fabrics (for all sizes)

⅝ yd. striped denim ticking
⅛ yd. red tonal print

Notions

Red sewing thread
Hand or machine sewing needle
Straight pins
1" wide elastic for the following:
  Size small 17"
  Size medium 18⅛"
  Size large 20"

Other Supplies

Patterns from the pattern sheet
  (pants front and back, cuffs)
Safety pin or elastic guide
Scissors
Iron and pressing surface

Cutting Instructions

FROM THE DENIM TICKING, CUT:
(4) Pants (2 fronts and 2 backs)
Note: *This fabric is directional, so be sure to cut all of the pants with the stripes facing in the same, upright direction.*

FROM THE RED TONAL PRINT, CUT:
(2) Cuffs

Directions

This project uses a ⅝" seam allowance.

1. With right sides together, stitch a pants front to a back at the side seams. Stitch the front to the back at the inner leg seams. Press. Repeat for the second front and back. ⬇

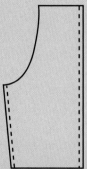

2. With right sides together, insert one pants leg inside of the other. Pin the curved center seam and stitch. If you are not using a serger, finish this seam as desired. Press.

3. Turn the pants inside out. Finish the top edge of the pants using a serger, or fold under ¼", and stitch in place.

4. Place the pants, inside out, on a flat pressing surface. Turn the top of the pants down 1¼" to form a casing for the elastic. Press.

5. Stitch the casing: Stitch around the top of the pants at the lower edge of the casing, leaving a 2" opening for inserting the elastic. Add a second row of stitches ¼" above the first, leaving a 2" opening for inserting the elastic.

6. Topstitch around the top of the pants, ⅛" from the folded edge.

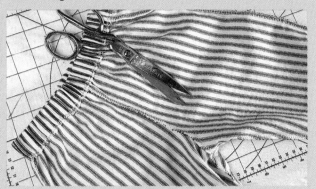

7. Attach an elastic guide or safety pin to one end of the elastic. Guide the elastic through the waistband. Overlap the edges, and stitch securely in place, using several rows of stitching. Adjust the fabric around the waistband and check the fit. Stitch the opening closed.

8. Add the cuffs: Select one cuff piece. Place right sides together, stitch along the short side, and press, forming a ring of fabric. Fold the fabric ring in half with wrong sides together and press. Repeat for the remaining cuff.

9. With the pants right-side out, insert the cuff into the pants leg, lining up the raw edges. Stitch around the edge. Turn the cuff to the outside and press in place. Repeat for the second cuff. Use red thread to stitch through the cuffs at each side seam to secure in place.

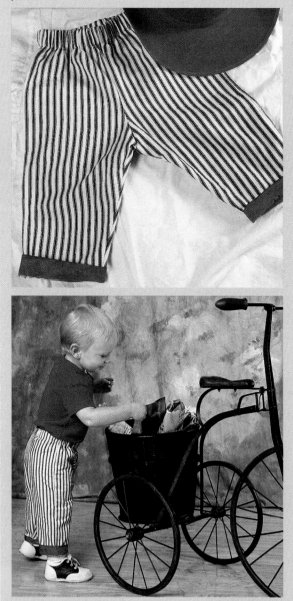

A size medium fits 20-month-old Eric, but he could easily wear a large as well. A large pants would be roomier and allow plenty of room for him to grow.

Patchwork Prairie Dress

Fabrics
1½ yd. red floral
1½ yd. blue gingham

Notions
3 white ⅜" buttons
Thread to match fabric
Hand or machine sewing needle
Straight pins

Other Supplies
Patterns from the pattern sheet
  (dress bodice front and back, sleeves)
Rotary cutter
Ruler
Cutting mat
Scissors
Water-soluble fabric marker
Iron and pressing surface

Cutting Instructions
FROM THE RED FLORAL, CUT:

Skirt
Size small cut:
(40) 2½" squares
(2) 3" x 44" strips for ruffle
Size medium, cut:
(40) 3" squares
(2) 4" x 44" strips for ruffle
Size large, cut:
(40) 3½" squares
(3) 5" x 44"strips for ruffle

Bodice
(1) Bodice front
(2) Bodice backs
(2) Sleeves

Tie
(1) 3" square

FROM THE BLUE GINGHAM, CUT:

Skirt
Size small, cut:
(40) 2½" squares
(2) 4" x 44" strips for ruffle
Size medium, cut:
(40) 3" squares
(2) 6" x 44" strips for ruffle
Size large, cut:
(40) 3½" squares
(3) 8" x 44" strips for ruffle

Bodice
(1) bodice front
(2) bodice backs

Tie
(1) 8" x 36" strip

Patchwork Prairie Dress reminds me of the pioneer style dresses worn by little girls a century ago. A dress from "back then" might have been constructed from an old quilt, feed sacks, or other simple fabric. I chose fun, bright colors, but you could substitute 1930s soft pastels if you prefer. The dress is designed to be long. If you prefer a shorter version, eliminate one or more rows of patchwork blocks from the skirt.

Directions

This project uses a ⅝" seam allowance.

1. Make the bodice: Stitch the red bodice backs to the bodice front, with right sides together, at the shoulder seams. Press. Repeat, using the blue gingham lining fabric.

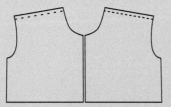

2. Place the blue gingham bodice piece right-side up on a flat work surface. Top with the red print bodice piece; right-side down. Pin at the neck and center back seams, and stitch. Clip the neck seams up to, but not through, the stitching. Turn right-side out and press. Topstitch along the neck and each side of the center back, ¼" from the edge.

3. Add the sleeves: Fold a sleeve piece in half lengthwise, wrong sides together, and stitch along the raw edges. Gather the top of the sleeve between the dots. Place the bodice with the floral side up, and pin the sleeve in place, matching up the raw edges. Stitch the sleeve. Repeat for the other side. Fold the sleeves into place and press.

4. Fold the bodice with right sides together. Stitch along each side, from the sleeve to the bottom edge. Turn to the right side and press.

5. Piece the skirt: Lay the skirt out on a large, flat surface — a large dining room table, or the floor works best. Arrange the red and blue squares into a rectangle, 16 squares wide by five squares tall. The squares should alternate between red and blue in a checkerboard pattern.

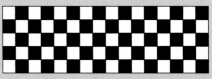

6. When you are happy with the layout, begin piecing. Start with the top row and sew the pieces together in order. Keep the right sides together. Once the row is sewn, place it back on your layout surface to keep the pieces in order. Repeat for each row. Once you have sewn all of the individual squares into rows, stitch the rows together.

7. Add the ruffles: Stitch the red ruffle strips, right sides together, to form a long chain. Repeat, using the blue ruffle strips.

8. Fold the red ruffle strips in half with wrong sides together and press. Stitch the raw edges together. Repeat, using the blue ruffle strips. Place the red ruffle strip on top of the blue ruffle strip. Stitch together along the raw edges.

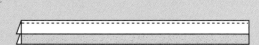

9. Gather the ruffle: Use a brightly-colored thread and gather by hand or machine along the raw edges. The ruffle will be thick.

10. Pin the ruffles to the skirt with right sides together. Match up the side edges and adjust the gathering to fit. Stitch in place. Press. Topstitch ¼" from the ruffles.

11. Fold the skirt with right sides together. Stitch along the short side, leaving a 5" unstitched portion at the top unruffled edge of the skirt. Turn right-side out and press. Gather the skirt along the top edge (the side with the 5" unstitched opening). Use a brightly-colored thread and gather by hand or machine.

12. Pin the skirt to the bodice with right sides together. Match up the back edges and side seams and adjust the gathering to fit. Stitch in place. Press.

13. Create the tie: Fold the 8" x 36" strip of blue gingham in half lengthwise, right sides together, and press. Stitch the raw edges together, leaving a 3" opening for turning. Turn right-side out and press. Fold the 3" red floral square in half, right sides together, and press. Stitch the raw edges together, leaving the ends open. Turn right-side out and press. Stitch the open edges together forming a ring. Turn and press.

14. Insert the blue gingham tie through the opening of the floral ring. Slide the ring to the center.

15. Pin the tie to the front of the dress. Stitch the floral ring in place at the center front of the waistline. Stitch the tie to each side seam to secure it.

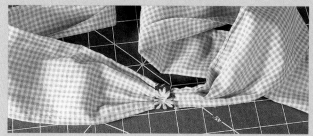

16. Mark and stitch the buttonholes as shown on the pattern. Mark and stitch the buttons as shown on the pattern.

3-year-old Ally wears a size large Patchwork Prairie Dress

Patchwork Prairie Headband

A headband like this one is so fast and easy to make. It's a great accent for just about any outfit. I really considered making a prairie style bonnet to go with the dress, but, in the end, decided it looked too "costumey." The headband adds a charming, finishing touch for the dress.

Fabrics

¼ yd. blue gingham
⅛ yd. red floral print

Notions

1 yd. 1" wide elastic
Thread to match fabric
Hand or machine sewing needle
Straight pins

Other Supplies

Rotary cutter
Ruler
Cutting mat
Water-soluble fabric marker
Scissors
Clear plastic template sheet
Iron and pressing surface
Safety pin or elastic guide
Tape measure

Cutting Instructions

FROM THE ELASTIC, CUT:
Cut the elastic using this figure as your guide:
Measure your child's head, then add 1".

FROM THE BLUE GINGHAM, CUT:
(1) 3" square
(1) 3" x 44" strip

FROM THE RED FLORAL, CUT:
(1) 5" x 10" rectangle
(1) 5" x 14" rectangle

Directions

This project uses a ⅜" seam allowance.

1. Make the band: With right sides together, stitch the 3"x 44" blue gingham strip along the 44" side. Turn right-side out and press.

2. Attach an elastic guide or safety pin to one end of the elastic. Guide the elastic through the headband tube. Overlap the elastic edges, and stitch securely in place, using several rows of stitching. Adjust the fabric around the headband and hand stitch the opening closed. ➥

3. Make the bow: With right sides together, stitch the 5" x 10" red floral rectangle along the 10" side. Turn right-side out and press. Fold this piece in half and stitch on the short side, forming a ring. Press, moving the seam to the middle of the ring. Repeat, using the 5" x 14" rectangle.

4. With right sides together, stitch the 3" blue gingham square along one edge. Press, moving the seam to the middle of the rectangle.

5. Assemble the bow: Stack the red floral piece on top of the gingham, keeping the seams facing the back. Wrap the center of the stacked bow pieces with thread. Pull it tight to gather the fabric at the center. Tie the thread into a knot to secure. Wrap the gingham strip around the bow piece and stitch in the back to secure.

Cowboy Bib

The denim for this project came from a recycled pair of bluejeans. Aged denim is the perfect accompaniment for the vintage-style cowboy print. The seam allowances on the bib are left exposed and form a decorative fringe around the edges of the bib. This is definitely a wash and wear project! The sturdy fabrics should hold up to plenty of use.

Fabrics
1 fat quarter vintage cowboy or other
    novelty fabric
14" square of denim
6" x 12" red flannel or cotton

Notions
1 white ¾" hook and loop tape dot
Thread to match fabric
Hand or machine sewing needle
Straight pins

Other Supplies
Pattern piece from the pattern sheet (bib)
Rotary cutter
Ruler
Cutting mat
Clear plastic template sheet
Pencil
Water-soluble fabric marker
Scissors
Iron and pressing surface

Cutting Instructions

FROM THE COWBOY PRINT, CUT:
(1) 10" square

FROM THE DENIM, CUT:
(1) 1" x 10" rectangle
(1) 12" square

FROM THE RED COTTON/FLANNEL, CUT:
(1) 5" x 10" rectangle

Directions

This project uses a ¼" seam allowance.

1. Make a plastic template: Use a pencil to trace the bib pattern onto the clear plastic template sheet. Cut out the bib template.

2. Make the bib front: With wrong sides together, stitch the 1" x 10" denim rectangle to the 10" square vintage cowboy print along the 10" edge.

3. With wrong sides together, stitch the 5" x 10" red cotton rectangle to the denim along the 10" edge.

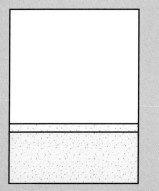

4. Cut two bibs: Place the pieced bib front fabric right-side up on a flat work surface. Place the plastic bib template on top of the fabric. Move the pattern around until you are happy with the way it will look. (Experiment with different areas of the fabric until you find the one you like.) Trace around the bib pattern with a water-soluble fabric marker and cut. Repeat, using the 12" denim square for the bib back.

5. Place the bib pieces wrong sides together. Sew all the way around the bib. Use scissors to snip the seam allowances every ¼" all the way around the bib and along the denim rectangle. Snip up to, but not over, the stitching. Wash and dry the bib.

6. Use fabric glue to attach the hook and loop tape dot to the neck portion of the bib. Let the glue dry for 48 hours before washing or wearing.
Note: *The neck edges overlap when the bib is worn.*

20-month-old Eric wears a size large bib.

Pillowcase Dress

Pillowcase dresses, like the one shown here, look simply adorable on little girls, and are oh-so-easy to make! Vintage pillowcases are very easy to find at a variety of venues. Remember, the opening of the pillowcase will become the hem of the dress, so crocheted or lace edges add a nice touch. Use a printed pillowcase like the one here, or choose one with vintage embroidery. If you happen to find a pair of matching pillowcases, make a set of matching "sister" dresses for siblings.

Fabric

1 standard-size pillowcase

Notions

1 yd. white ⅜" bias tape (use white,
  or choose a color to match your pillowcase)
Thread to match fabric
Straight pins
Hand or machine sewing needle

Other Supplies

Patterns from the pattern sheet (dress, armhole)
Water-soluble fabric marker
Iron and pressing surface   Ruler
Safety pin or elastic guide   Scissors

Cutting Instructions

FROM THE BIAS TAPE, CUT:
(2) 18" pieces

Directions

This project uses a ⅝" seam allowance.

1. Make a plastic template: Use a pencil to trace the armhole pattern onto the clear plastic template sheet. Cut out the armhole template.

2. Cut the pillowcase: Measure and mark the dress pattern length on the pillowcase. Cut across the pillowcase on the marked line.
For size small, mark and cut 18" from the hem.
For size medium, mark and cut 21½" from the hem.
For size large, mark and cut 25" from the hem.

3. Place the pillowcase right-side up on a flat work surface. Mark and cut an armhole from each side of the dress.

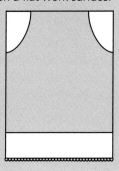

4. Stitch each 18" piece of bias tape, with right sides together, along the length. Using bias tape is a timesaver for this project. The tape has plenty of give, which makes it ideal for tying into bows. Be sure not to stretch the tape as you sew.

5. Turn the armhole openings under ¼" and press. Turn the armhole openings under ¼" again. Press and stitch in place.

6. Make the casing: Turn the pillowcase inside out. Turn the top front of the dress down ¼", with wrong sides together and press. Turn under 1", then press and stitch in place. The edges will not match up perfectly at the sides due to the curved shape of the armholes. Repeat for the back of the dress.

7. Topstitch ⅛" from the folded edge of the dress front. Repeat for the dress back.

8. Attach an elastic guide or safety pin to one end of the bias tape. Guide the tape through the dress front casing. Repeat for the back.

9. Tie a bow at each shoulder. The fabric will gather along the front and back neck. If the child is present, try the dress on to check the fit. Remove the garment, keeping the bows tied (or mark their placement with a water-soluble fabric marker). Stitch the front and back ties securely in place at each casing opening. You can tie and untie the drawstrings of the dress, but you will not be able to remove them. This is an important safety step for this garment.

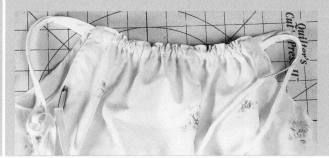

Sugar and Spice Baby Quilt

I made this quilt with painted blocks. If you prefer, you could embroider each block instead. Use the colors suggested for painting, or embroider in red tones for a striking redwork quilt. Finished size is 36" square.

Fabrics

½ yd. white cotton (painted blocks)
6 fat quarters 1930s reproduction prints:
  mint green, yellow, purple, blue, pink, ivory
  (pieced blocks)
½ yd. blue 1930s reproduction print (border)
½ yd. green 1930s reproduction print (binding)
1 yd. blue 1930s reproduction print (backing)

Notions

Thread to match fabric
Hand or machine sewing needle
Straight pins
1 yd. cotton quilt batting

Other Supplies

Black fabric marker (permanent and waterproof)
Acrylic craft paints in the following colors:
  yellow, red, green, tan, blue, lavender, black,
  beige
Small No. 10 (or smaller) watercolor paintbrush
Paper or foam plate or tray
Rotary cutter
Ruler
Cutting mat
Scissors
Iron and pressing surface

Cutting Instructions

Note: *Wash and dry all fabrics before cutting.*

FROM THE WHITE COTTON, CUT:
(5) 9" squares

**FROM THE BLUE REPRODUCTION BORDER
PRINT, CUT:**
(4) 2½" x 30" strips

FROM EACH FAT QUARTER, CUT:
(12) 2½" squares

Directions

This project uses a ¼" seam allowance.

1. Trace the designs: Use the fabric marker to trace each design onto a 9" white fabric square, centering carefully. Allow the marker to dry completely.

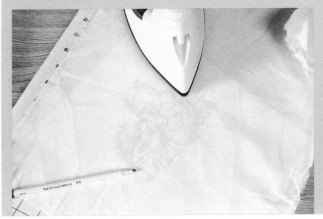

COLORING GUIDE:

This is a guide to the colors used in the sample. Feel free to modify as you'd like, to color schemes that suit your taste or décor.

Girl with Geese:
Yellow: hair, slip, goose beaks and feet, inside of feed pan
Green: dress, socks, ground, hair ribbon
Beige: skin, geese
Black: shoes, feed pan

Croquet girl:
Tan: hair, ball, mallet
Lavender: dress, socks, stripe on ball and mallet
Beige: skin
Green: ground
Black: shoes

Girl with Bunny:
Tan: hair, basket, bunny
Red: hair ribbon, dress, socks
Green: carrot tops, ground
Orange: carrots (mix a bit of red into the yellow)
Black: shoes
Beige: skin

Tea Party:
Tan: hair, table, chair, doll hair
Blue: hair ribbons, dress, doll dress
Red: dishes
Black: shoes
Beige: skin, doll
Green: ground

Girl reading:
Tan: hair, dog
Yellow: dress, ribbon, socks
Red: book cover, leash
Beige: pages, skin
Black: shoes
Green: ground

2. Paint the 9" squares. Pour a small amount of each color paint (about the size of a dime) onto a paper or foam plate. Use water to thin the paint until it is a very thin wash. Practice on a scrap of fabric until you have the color you want. The squares in the sample were painted with a mixture of paint and water ratio of 8:1 (8 parts water to 1 part paint). Use the paintbrush and acrylic paint to color in each square, coloring book style. Use the coloring guide, or choose your own colors. To shade, paint an area once, allow it to dry, and paint it again with the same color. Leave white areas unpainted.

IMPORTANT: You must heat set the paint once it has dried by pressing with a hot iron. This allows your project to be laundered. Once painted and set, trim each 9" square to an 8½" square, carefully centering the design.

3. Lay your quilt out on a large, flat surface — a large dining room table, or the floor works best. Arrange the 2½" squares into groups of 16 pieces, with four squares across and four squares down. Vary the placement and colors to create good variety in your blocks. You will have some squares left over. Discard them or use them for another purpose.

4. When you are happy with the layout of the blocks, begin piecing. Start with the top row of four squares. With right sides together, sew the squares together. Press. Repeat for each row of four squares, keeping the pieces in order. With right sides together, sew the four rows together. Press. Once the block is sewn, place it back on your layout surface to keep the blocks in order. Repeat for each block.

5. Lay out the blocks: Lay out the painted blocks and the pieced blocks as shown on the photo. Stitch together by row, then assemble the rows.

6. Add the border: Attach the border strips to the sides. Press and trim. Attach the border strips to the top and bottom. Press and trim.

7. Layer the backing (face down), batting and quilt top (face up). Baste. Machine or hand quilt around each painted block and diagonally through each pieced block. Add the binding, finishing to a ½" finished binding width.

Hankie Bonnet

Choose a vintage ladies handkerchief with a lacy edge to make this heirloom bonnet. I love finding new uses for vintage pieces! This bonnet is an ideal project for a christening or other special event. A 10" hankie will fit most babies up to 3 months. For larger babies, choose a larger handkerchief.

Fabric (for all sizes)

10" or 12" square vintage handkerchief

Notions

½ yd. matching ¼" satin ribbon
1 yd. matching ½" satin ribbon
Thread to match fabric
Hand or machine sewing needle
Rosettes (optional)

Other Supplies

Scissors
Iron and pressing surface
Safety pin or elastic guide

Directions

1. Fold the handkerchief in half with wrong sides together, and press.

2. Stitch across the handkerchief ½" from the folded edge to form a casing.

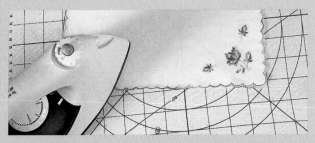

3. Attach an elastic guide or safety pin to one end of the ¼" ribbon. Guide the ribbon through the casing.

4. Gather the casing to create the back of the bonnet, and tie the ribbon in a knot. Tie a bow.

5. Fold the front of the bonnet back 1". Press, then stitch in place.

6. Cut two 14" pieces of ½" ribbon. Hand stitch a ribbon to each side of the bonnet. Hand stitch a rosette on top of each ribbon end. You can add additional rosettes, if your prefer.

The most popular, longest enduring baby trend of the moment is "Upscale Whimsical." Designers like Baby Lulu®, Wendy Bellissimo®, Hanna Andersson® and Lilly Pulitzer® all have great upscale whimsical lines. Bright, mixed colors, fun and funky silhouettes, crisp cottons and painterly images are the hallmarks of upscale whimsy. "Retired" items often sell for twice their original retail price on eBay and new fashion lines are eagerly awaited. Upscale whimsical works for infants of both genders and for little girls of all ages.

Chapter 5 Upscale Whimsical

Floral Sundress & Floppy Sun Hat

Showcase a great fabric using this simple sundress pattern. The dress front is solid, so you can use a large-scale print like this sharp black and white floral. This dress can also be worn as a jumper; just add a lightweight T-shirt underneath. 6-month-old Cassie wears a size small sundress.

Floral Sundress:

Fabrics
1 yd. black-white floral print
¼ yd. black-white gingham
½ yd. black cotton (facings)

Notions
2 black gingham ½" fabric-covered buttons
   (See page 125 for instructions for covering
   buttons)
Thread to match fabric
Straight pins
Hand or machine sewing needle

Other Supplies
Patterns from the pattern sheet (sundress/jumper
   front and back, front and back facings)
Rotary cutter
Ruler
Cutting mat
Scissors
Water-soluble fabric marker
Iron and pressing surface

Cutting Instructions
FROM THE BLACK-WHITE FLORAL, CUT:
(1) Jumper/sundress front
(1) Jumper/sundress back

FROM THE BLACK COTTON, CUT:
(1) Front facing
(1) Back facing

FROM THE BLACK-WHITE GINGHAM, CUT:
Size infants or small (2) 4" x 36" strips for ruffle
Size medium (2) 4" x 40" strips
Size large (2) 5" x 44" strips

Directions
This project uses a ⅝" seam allowance.

1. Place the dress front, right-side up, on a flat work surface. Top with the front facing, right-side down. Pin at the neck, shoulders and armholes and stitch. Clip the seams up to, but not through, the stitching. Turn right-side out and press. Repeat, attaching the back facing to the dress back.

2. Topstitch along the neck, armholes and shoulders of each piece, ¼" from the edge.

3. With right sides together, stitch the dress front to the back along the sides. Turn right-side out and press.

4. Stitch the short edges of the ruffle strips with right sides together, forming a ring of fabric. Press. Fold the ruffle strip in half, wrong sides together, and press. Stitch the raw edges together. Gather the ruffle: Use a brightly-colored thread and gather by hand or machine along the raw edges.

5. Pin the ruffle to the bottom of the dress, right sides together. Match up the side edges and adjust the gathering to fit. Stitch in place. Press. Topstitch ¼" from the ruffles.

6. Mark and stitch the buttonholes as shown on the pattern. Mark and securely hand stitch the buttons. See page 11 for important safety instructions for adding buttons to children's clothing.

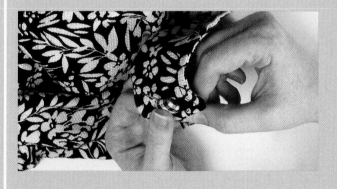

I make a hat or hair accessory to match almost every outfit I make for my girls. It uses up leftover fabrics, and adds an attractive finishing touch as well. Hats like the Floppy Sun Hat also provide some shade — protection from the damaging rays of the sun in the summer months.

Directions

This project uses a ⅜" seam allowance.

1. With right sides together, stitch the curved edges of two hat top pieces together. Snip seams and press. Repeat, using the remaining hat top pieces.

2. With right sides together, stitch the hat top pieces together, forming a "bowl" of fabric. Turn right-side out and press.

3. With right sides together, stitch the short ends of the floral brim pieces together, forming a ring of fabric. Turn right-side out and press. Repeat, using the black hat brim pieces.

4. With right sides together, stitch the floral brim pieces to the black brim pieces along the outer edges. Snip the seams. Turn right-side out and press.

5. Gather the hat top: Use a brightly-colored thread and gather loosely by hand or machine along the raw edges. With the right sides together, baste the hat to the brim. Match up the raw edges and adjust the gathering to fit. Stitch in place. Press.

Floppy Sun Hat:

Fabrics
½ yd. black-white floral print
½ yd. black cotton (lining)

Notions
Thread to match fabric
Hand or machine sewing needle
Straigh pins

Other Supplies
Patterns from the pattern sheet (hat, brim)
Scissors
Iron and pressing surface

Cutting Instructions
FROM THE BLACK-WHITE FLORAL, CUT:
(4) Hat tops
(2) Brims

FROM THE BLACK LINING, CUT:
(2) Brims

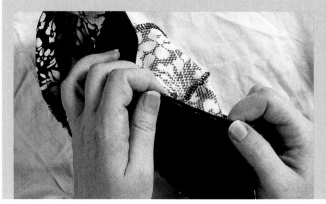

Cha-Cha-Cha Rumba Shorts

Yes, you can combine bright pink and green! Just make sure the colors are of the same intensity, or choose coordinating prints like the ones shown here. The ruffles add a touch of fun without being "too much." These perky shorts are as fun to make as they are to wear! Taylor just turned 3, and wears a size large shorts.

Fabrics

½ yd. bright pink butterfly print
½ yd. bright green stripe

Notions

Thread to match fabric
Hand or machine sewing needle
Straight pins
2 pieces of ⅜" wide elastic for the following:
   Size small 17"
   Size medium 18½"
   Size large 20"

Other Supplies

Pattern from the pattern sheet (shorts)
Scissors
Iron and pressing surface
Safety pin or elastic guide

Cutting Instructions

FROM THE BRIGHT PINK PRINT, CUT:
(4) Shorts
Size infants or small (2) 3" x 30" strips for ruffle
Size medium or large (2) 4" x 36" strips for ruffle

Directions

This project uses a ⅝" seam allowance.

1. Place one shorts piece right-side up on a flat work surface. Top with a second piece, right-side down. Pin together along the long straight side and stitch. Press open. Repeat, using the remaining shorts pieces.

2. Make the ruffles: Fold a ruffle strip in half lengthwise, wrong sides together, and press. Stitch the raw edges together.

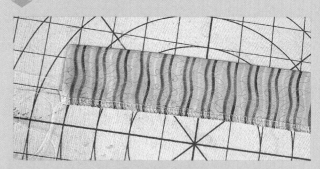

3. Gather the ruffle: Use a brightly-colored thread and gather by hand or machine along the raw edges. Repeat, for a total of two ruffles.

4. Stitch the ruffles to the bottom of the shorts pieces, right sides together, and matching up the raw edges. Press and topstitch.

5. Fold a shorts piece with right sides together. Pin along the short straight side and stitch. Press. Repeat, using the remaining shorts piece.

6. Assemble the shorts: With right sides together, place one shorts piece inside the other. Stitch along the curved center seam. Turn the shorts right-side out and press.

7. Turn the shorts inside out. Finish the top edge of the shorts using a serger, or fold under ¼" and stitch in place.

8. Fold the top edge of the shorts down 1½" and press. Stitch all the way around the top of the shorts, ⅛" from the folded edge.

9. Stitch around the top of the shorts, ¾" from the folded edge, leaving a 3" opening to insert the elastic. Attach an elastic guide or safety pin to one end of an elastic strip. Guide the elastic through the waistband. Overlap the edges, and stitch securely in place, using several rows of stitching. Adjust the fabric around the waistband, then check the fit. Complete the stitching of this row, stretching the elastic as needed as you work.

10. Stitch around the top of the shorts, 1½" from the folded edge, leaving a 3" opening to insert the elastic. Attach an elastic guide or safety pin to one end of an elastic strip. Guide the elastic through the waistband. Overlap the edges, and stitch securely in place, using several rows of stitching. Adjust the fabric around the waistband, then check the fit. Stitch the opening closed.

Cha-Cha-Cha Rumba Top

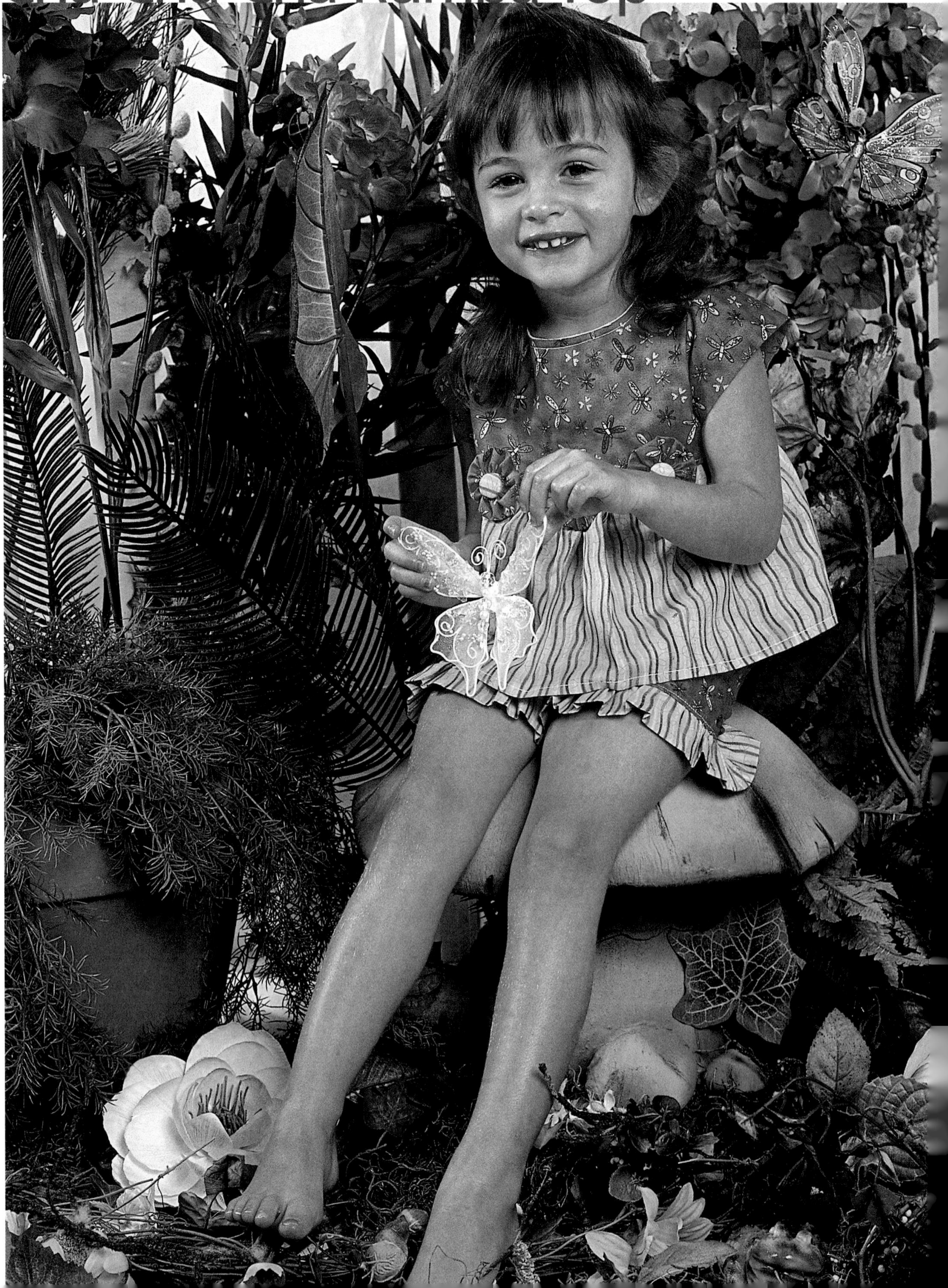

I love the wild print used for this top! Make it to wear with jeans or denim shorts, or make the matching pair of shorts on page 85. Either way, this is a real eye-catcher, and it's sure to be one of your little girl's favorite outfits!

Ally is 3 and wears the Rumba set in a size large. To make a hair ornament like the one Ally is wearing, make one more yo-yo/button piece and securely stitch it to a knitted ponytail "O."

Fabrics
½ yd. bright pink butterfly print
½ yd. bright green stripe
½ yd. white fabric (lining)

Notions
4 white ⅜" buttons
Thread to match fabric
Hand or machine sewing needle
Straight pins
3 green stripe ½" fabric-covered buttons (See page 125 for directions for covering buttons)

Other Supplies
Patterns from the pattern sheet (bodice front and back, sleeve, large yo-yo)
Water-soluble fabric marker
Scissors
Iron and pressing surface
Cutting mat
Rotary cutter

Cutting Instructions
FROM THE PINK PRINT, CUT:
(1) Bodice front
(2) Bodice backs
(2) Sleeves
(3) Large yo-yo circles

FROM THE GREEN STRIPE, CUT:
Size infants or small (2) 4" x 36" strips
Size medium or large (2) 5" x 44" strips

FROM THE WHITE LINING, CUT:
(1) Bodice front
(2) Bodice backs

Directions

This project uses a ⅝" seam allowance.

1. Make the bodice: Stitch the butterfly print bodice backs, right sides together, to the bodice front at the shoulder seams. Press. Repeat, using the white lining fabric.

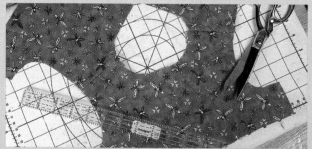

2. Place the white bodice piece right-side up on a flat work surface. Top with the print bodice piece, right-side down. Pin at the neck and center back seams, and stitch. Clip the neck seams up to, but not through, the stitching. Turn right-side out and press. Topstitch along the neck and each side of the center back, ¼" from the edge.

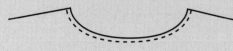

3. Add the sleeves: Fold a sleeve piece in half lengthwise with wrong sides together. Stitch along the raw edges. Gather the top of the sleeve between the dots.

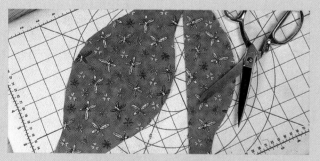

4. Place the bodice with the butterfly side up and pin the sleeve in place, matching up the raw edges. Stitch the sleeve. Repeat for the other side. Fold the sleeves in place and press.

5. Fold the bodice with right sides together. Stitch along each side, from the sleeve to the bottom edge. Turn to the right side and press.

6. Place the two green stripe pieces with right sides together. Stitch along the short side. Serge or zigzag stitch 1/4" from the top long edge to finish. Press.

7. Fold the shirt bottom piece in half, right sides together. Stitch the short sides together, leaving a 3" unstitched portion at one end of the shirt. Turn right-side out. Press.

8. Gather the top along the top portion (the side with the 3" unstitched opening).

9. Pin the shirt bottom to the bodice with right sides together. Match up the side edges and adjust the gathering to fit. Stitch in place. Press. Topstitch ¼" from the seam.

10. Gather around the edge of a yo-yo circle, and pull tight, forming a pouch. Flatten and press. Repeat for the remaining two yo-yos.

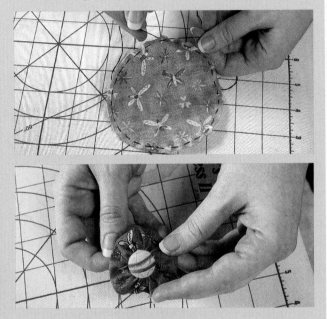

11. Securely hand stitch the yo-yos in place on the front of the bodice, spacing them evenly across the bodice front. Top each yo-yo with a covered button. Stitch in place through all the layers. See page 11 for important safety instructions for adding buttons to children's clothing.

12. Mark and stitch the buttonholes at the back, as shown on the pattern. Mark and stitch the buttons, as shown on the pattern.

Kerchief

I made this kerchief in denim, so it works with a variety of outfits. This one-size-fits-all kerchief will work best on older babies and toddlers. The kerchief sports a bow at the back of the head, and may be uncomfortable for babies who are unable to sit up.

Fabric

½ yd. denim (new or recycled)

Notions

Thread to match fabric
Straight pins
Hand or machine sewing needle (Size 16 or 18 jeans needle for thick fabrics such as denim or canvas

Other Supplies

Rotary cutter
Ruler
Cutting mat
Water-soluble fabric marker
Scissors
Iron and pressing surface

Cutting Instructions

FROM THE DENIM, CUT:
(1) 14" square
(1) 1" x 24" strip

Directions

This project uses a ¼" seam allowance.

1. With wrong sides together, fold the 14" square in half diagonally, forming a triangle. Sew all the way around the triangle. Use scissors to snip the raw edges every ¼", all the way around the triangle. Snip up to, but not over, the stitching.

2. With right sides together, place the denim 1" x 24" strip along the folded edge of the triangle. Center the triangle on the denim strip. Stitch in place using a ¼" seam allowance. Open and press.

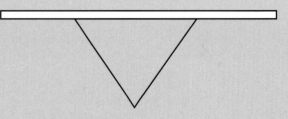

3. Finish the long edge of the tie with a serger, or turn under ¼" and stitch. Fold the tie over the edge of the kerchief and stitch in place. Stitch along the sides of the tie to secure. Tie a knot at the end of each tie.

4. Wash and dry the kerchief to fringe the denim.

Rainforest Pants

Look closely at this fabric and you will see brightly-colored frogs, lizards, birds and bugs. The variety of colors in the print allows the finished pants to coordinate with just about any brightly-colored top. Substitute a red, purple, or bright green cuff if you don't like the yellow.

Fabrics (for all sizes)
⅝ yd. rainforest print
⅛ yd. bright yellow tonal print

Notions
Thread to match fabric
Straight pins
Hand or machine sewing needle
1" wide elastic for the following:
   Size infants and small 17"
   Size medium 18½"
   Size large 20"

Other Supplies
Patterns from the pattern sheet
   (pants front and back, cuffs)
Scissors
Iron and pressing surface
Safety pin or elastic guide

Cutting Instructions
FROM THE RAINFOREST PRINT, CUT:
(4) Pants (2 fronts and 2 backs)

FROM THE YELLOW PRINT, CUT:
(2) Cuffs

Directions

1. This project uses a ⅝" seam allowance. With right sides together, stitch a pants front to a back at side seams. Stitch the front to the back at the inner leg seams. Press. Repeat for the second front and back.

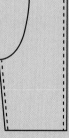

2. With right sides together, insert one pants leg inside of the other. Pin the curved center seam and stitch. If you are not using a serger, finish this seam as desired. Press.

3. Turn the pants inside out. Finish the top opening of the pants using a serger, or fold under ¼" and stitch in place.

4. Place the pants, inside out, on a flat pressing surface. Turn the top of the pants down 1¼" to form a casing for the elastic. Press.

5. Stitch the casing: Stitch around the top of the pants at the lower edge of the casing, leaving a 2" opening for inserting the elastic. Add a second row of stitches ¼" above the first, leaving a 2" opening for inserting the elastic.

6. Stitch around the top of the pants, ⅛" from the folded edge.

7. Attach an elastic guide or safety pin to one end of the elastic. Guide the elastic through the waistband. Overlap the edges, and stitch securely in place, using several rows of stitching. Adjust the fabric around the waistband, then check the fit. Stitch the opening closed.

8. Add the cuffs: Select one cuff piece. Place right sides together, stitch along the short side, and press, forming a ring of fabric. Fold the fabric ring in half with wrong sides together. Press.

9. With the pants right-side out, insert the cuff into the pants leg, lining up the raw edges. Stitch around the edge. Turn the cuff to the outside and press in place. Use yellow thread to stitch through the cuffs at each side seam to secure in place.

Whimsical Striped Bib

I like to save small scraps from finished projects. You never know when you can find a use for them — as an appliqué, as part of a scrappy quilt, or on a bib, as shown here.

Fabrics

1 fat quarter bright pink polka dot
1 fat quarter butterfly print
1 fat eighth pink-white stripe

Notions

1 purchased 1¼" tall embroidered flower
    appliqué
1 purchased 1½" wide embroidered butterfly
    appliqué
1 white ¾" hook and loop tape dot
12" floral ½" woven ribbon
Thread to match fabric
Hand or machine sewing needle

Other Supplies

Pattern from the pattern sheet (bib)
Rotary cutter
Cutting mat
Clear plastic template sheet
Water-soluble fabric marker   Ruler
Fabric glue   Pencil
Iron and pressing surface   Scissors

Cutting Instructions

FROM THE PINK POLKA DOT, CUT:
(1) 10" square

FROM THE PINK-WHITE STRIPE, CUT:
(1) 5" x 10" rectangle

FROM THE BUTTERFLY PRINT, CUT:
(1) 15" square

Directions

This project uses a ⅜" seam allowance.

1. Make a plastic template: Use a pencil to trace the bib pattern onto the clear plastic template sheet. Cut out the bib template.

2. Make the bib front: With right sides together, stitch the 5" x 10" pink stripe rectangle to the 10" square polka dot. Press. Stitch the ribbon onto the front of the bib, covering the seam. Stitch the floral appliqué on top of the ribbon in the center front of the bib.

3. Cut two bibs: Place the bib front fabric and the 15" butterfly print, right-sides up, on a flat work surface. Place the bib template on top of the fabrics. Move the template pattern around until you are happy with the way it will look. (Experiment with different areas of the fabric until you find the one you like.) Trace around the bib pattern with a water-soluble fabric marker. Cut out the bib pieces.

4. Stitch the butterfly in place at the lower right corner of the butterfly print bib, about 1½" from the edge.

5. Place the bib pieces right sides together. Sew all the way around the bib, leaving a 3" opening for turning. Use scissors to snip the seam allowances every ¼" along the curves. Snip up to, but not  over, the stitching. Turn the bib right-side out and press. Hand stitch the opening closed.

6. Use fabric glue to attach the hook and loop tape dot to the neck portion of the bib. Let the glue dry for 48 hours before washing or wearing.
Note: The neck edges overlap when the bib is worn.

Lemon Drop Shirt

The pants that go with this shirt are a little on the wild side, so I chose to make this clean and simple. A strip of rickrack and a hint of chenille are all the ornamentation this top needs to shine.

Fabrics

½ yd. cotton lemon-print
6" square white chenille

Notions

1 yd. black jumbo rickrack trim
1 lemon-print ½" fabric-covered button
   (See page 125 for directions for covering
   buttons)
1 yd. black ⅜" bias tape
Straight pins
Thread to match fabric
Hand or machine sewing thread

Other Supplies

Patterns from the pattern sheet
   (small and large yo-yo, armhole)
Rotary cutter
Ruler
Cutting mat
Fabric marker
Scissors
Iron and pressing surface
Safety pin or elastic guide

Cutting Instructions

FROM THE LEMON-PRINT, CUT:
Size infants (2) 13" squares
Size small (2) 14½" squares
Size medium (2) 16" squares
Size large (2) 18" squares

FROM THE CHENILLE, CUT:
Size infants or small (1) small yo-yo
Size medium or large (1) large yo-yo

Directions

This project uses a ⅝" seam allowance.

1. Make a plastic template: Use a pencil to trace the armhole pattern onto the clear plastic template sheet. Cut out the armhole template.

2. Place the square lemon-print pieces right sides together. Sew along two side edges, making a tube of fabric. Turn right-side out and press.

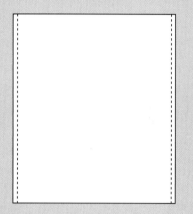

3. Place the fabric tube right-side up on a flat work surface. Mark and cut an armhole for each side of the shirt.

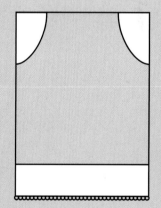

4. Stitch the black bias tape along the length with right sides together. Turn right-side out and press. Using bias tape is a timesaver for this project. The tape has plenty of give, which makes it ideal for tying into bows. Be sure not to stretch the tape as you sew. Cut the sewn bias tape strip into two 18" pieces for size medium or large, two 16" pieces for size small, or two 14" pieces for infants.

5. Turn the armhole openings under ¼" and press. Turn them under ¼", press, then stitch in place.

6. Turn the shirt inside out. Turn the top front of the shirt down ¼" and press. Turn under 1", press, then stitch in place. The edges will not match up perfectly at the sides due to the curved shape of the armholes. Repeat for the back of the shirt.

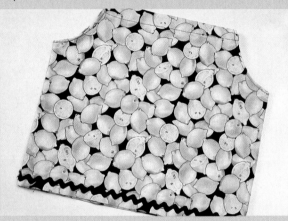

7. Finish the bottom hem with a serger, or turn under ¼" and stitch in place. Turn under 1" and stitch in place. Stitch the jumbo rickrack in place on top of the hemstitching. The rickrack is large enough to stitch right through the center of it, using matching thread. There is no need to follow the individual zigzags as you stitch.

8. Attach an elastic guide or safety pin to one end of the bias tape. Guide the tape through the front casing. Repeat for the back.

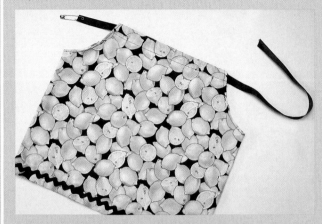

9. Tie a bow at each shoulder. The fabric will gather along the front and back neck. If the child is present, try the shirt on to check the fit. Remove the garment, keeping the bows tied (or mark their placement with a water-soluble fabric marker). Stitch the front and back neck ties securely in place at each casing opening. You can tie and untie the drawstrings of the shirt, but you will not be able to remove them. This is an important safety step for this garment.

10. Gather around the edge of a yo-yo circle, and pull tight, forming a pouch. Flatten and press.

11. Securely hand stitch the yo-yo in place on the front of the shirt. Top the yo-yo with a fabric-covered button. Stitch in place through all layers. See page 11 for important safety instructions for adding buttons to children's clothing.

These pants are pretty simple to make, but have tons of cute details. Wear the pants alone, or with the matching Lemon Drop Shirt. If lemons are not your thing, feel free to substitute another fun, bright print.

Fabrics (for all sizes)

⅜ yd. cotton lemon-print
⅝ yd. chenille (The chenille used in this project was cut from an old bedspread. You can use vintage or new chenille for these pants.)

Notions

1" wide elastic for the following:
   Size infants and small 17"
   Size medium 18½"
   Size large 20"
For size medium or large only:
   2 lemon-print ½" fabric-covered buttons
   (See page 125 for directions for covering
   buttons)
Thread to match fabric
Hand or machine sewing needle
Straight pins

Other Supplies

Patterns from the pattern sheet
   (pants front and back, yo-yo)
Scissors
Iron and pressing surface
Safety pin or elastic guide

Cutting Instructions

Note: *If your fabric is directional, cut all of the pants pieces with the pattern facing in the same, upright direction.*
Infants or small — omit yo-yos (Babies in this age group would be very likely to lie on the ground, and could possibly chew on the pants legs, making the yo-yos a possible safety hazard, regardless of how securely they are stitched.)

FROM THE CHENILLE, CUT:
(4) Pants (2 fronts and 2 backs)
Size medium or large (2) large yo-yos

FROM THE LEMON-PRINT, CUT:

Ruffles
Size infants or small (2) 4½" x 22" strips
Size medium (2) 5" x 24" strips
Size large (2) 6" x 28" strips

Directions

This project uses a ⅝" seam allowance.

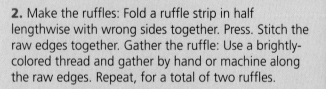

1. With right sides together, stitch a pants front to a back at side seams. Stitch the front to the back at the inner leg seams. Press. Repeat for the second front and back.

2. Make the ruffles: Fold a ruffle strip in half lengthwise with wrong sides together. Press. Stitch the raw edges together. Gather the ruffle: Use a brightly-colored thread and gather by hand or machine along the raw edges. Repeat, for a total of two ruffles.

3. Stitch the ruffles to the bottom of the pants pieces, with right sides together, matching up the raw edges. Press and topstitch. The ruffles will be very full and will stick out quite a bit when you finish the topstitching.

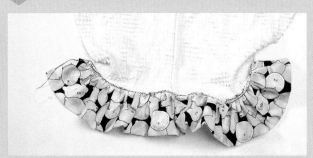

4. Stitch the pants front to the back at the inner leg seams, including the ruffle. Press. Repeat for the second front and back.

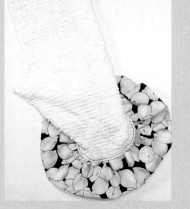

5. With right sides together, insert one pants leg inside of the other. Pin the curved center seam and stitch. If you are not using a serger, finish this seam as desired. Press.

6. Turn the pants inside out. Finish the top edge of the pants using a serger, or fold under 1¼" and stitch in place.

7. Place the pants, inside out, on a flat pressing surface. Turn the top of the pants down 1¼" to form a casing for the elastic. Press.

8. Stitch the casing: Stitch around the top of the pants at the lower edge of the casing, leaving a 2" opening for inserting the elastic. Add a second row of stitches ¼" above the first, leaving a 2" opening for inserting the elastic.

9. Attach an elastic guide or safety pin to one end of the elastic. Guide the elastic through the waistband. Overlap the edges, and stitch securely in place, using several rows of stitching. Adjust the fabric around the waistband, then check the fit. Stitch the opening closed.

10. For larger sizes only: Gather around the edge of a yo-yo circle, and pull tight, forming a pouch. Flatten and press. Repeat for the remaining yo-yo.

11. Securely hand stitch the yo-yos in place on the front of the pants ruffle. Top each yo-yo with a covered button. Stitch in place through all the layers. See page 11 for important safety instructions for adding buttons to children's clothing.

The clean lines and bright, clear colors that are hallmarks of Scandinavian design carry-over well for baby wear. Projects in this chapter are made using bright, snuggly fleece or cotton knits and are equally suited to girls or boys. Fleece is very easy to work with and comes in a great variety of colors and patterns. Blanket stitching, fun color combinations and simple embellishments complete the look.

Chapter 6 Winter Brights

Pink Flowers Jacket

One of the reasons I enjoy working with fleece, is its versatility. You can cut the fleece into whatever shape you like and simply blanket stitch the edges for a nice, finished look. I added a scalloped hem to the fleece Pink Flowers Jacket and made some simple flower appliqués for the pockets. This jacket is unlined, but if you prefer a lining, add one using a complementary shade of fleece, and follow the directions for the Reversible Blue Jacket on page 114.

Fabrics

1 yd. pale pink fleece

¼ yd. white fleece (¼ yard will be enough fleece to complete both the jacket and the hat project found on page 111)

10" square pale blue fleece

8" square pale green fleece

Notions

I skein embroidery floss to match the pink fabric

Tapestry needle

White sewing thread

Straight pins

Hand or machine sewing needle

Other Supplies

Patterns from the pattern sheet (jacket front and back, cuff, large and small yo-yo, leaf, scallop)

Pencil

Clear plastic template sheet

Water-soluble fabric marker

Scissors

Iron and pressing surface

Cutting Instructions

FROM THE PINK FLEECE, CUT:

(2) Jacket fronts

(1) Jacket back

Jacket pockets:

    Infants and small (2) 3" squares

    Medium and large sizes (2) 4" squares

FROM THE WHITE FLEECE, CUT:

(2) Cuffs

(2) Large yo-yos

FROM THE BLUE FLEECE, CUT:

(2) Small yo-yos

FROM THE GREEN FLEECE, CUT:

(4) Leaves

Directions

This project uses a ⅝" seam allowance.

1. Make a plastic template: Use a pencil to trace the scallop pattern onto the clear plastic template sheet. Cut out the scallop template.

2. With right sides together, stitch the jacket fronts to the jacket backs at the shoulder seams. Stitch each side seam from the bottom of the jacket to the end of the sleeve.

3. Place the jacket right-side up on a flat work surface. Open up the jacket front and place the scallop template on top of the fabric. Line up the scalloped edge of the template with the bottom edge of the jacket. Trace around the scallop pattern with a water-soluble fabric marker. Repeat, working your way from one end of the jacket to the other.

4. Cut along the marked line.

5. Use six strands of pink floss and the tapestry needle to blanket stitch along the scalloped edge. Repeat, to blanket stitch along the jacket neckline.

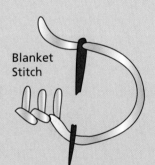

Blanket Stitch

6. Select a white cuff piece. Place right sides together and stitch along the short side. Press, forming a ring of fabric. Fold the fabric ring in half, wrong sides together, and press. Repeat for the remaining cuff.

7. With the jacket right-side out, insert the cuff into the sleeve opening, lining up the raw edges. Stitch around the edge. Turn the cuff to the outside and press in place. Use white thread to stitch through the cuffs at each side seam to secure in place. Repeat for the remaining sleeve cuff.

8. Make the flowers: Gather around the edge of a white yo-yo circle and pull tight, forming a pouch. Flatten and press. Repeat for the remaining white and blue yo-yos.

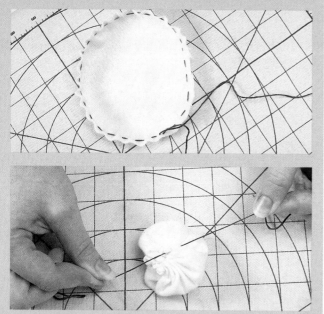

9. Gather across the straight edge of a green leaf and pull tight. Tie to secure. Repeat for the remaining leaf.

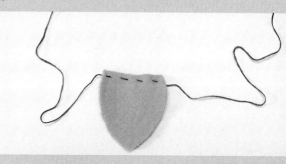

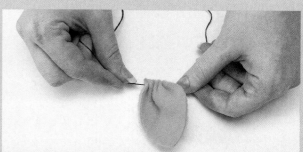

10. Securely hand stitch two leaves in place on each pocket piece. Top with a white yo-yo, then a blue yo-yo. Securely stitch in place through all layers. See page 11 for important safety instructions for adding appliqués to children's clothing.

11. Use six strands of pink floss and the tapestry needle to blanket stitch a pocket to each side of the jacket front.

Pink Skirt

This is such a simple project — just a tube with a waistband! The scalloped hem adds a pretty touch that matches the other pieces in this group. If you live in a warmer climate, like I do, a fleece skirt with a pair of tights is ideal winter garb for your little one. If you are in a colder area, and prefer something more substantial, make a pair of pants instead. To make pants, follow the directions on page 116 and replace the blue and green fleece with pink and white.

Fabric (for all sizes)

⅜ yd. pale pink fleece

Notions

1 yd. 1" wide elastic
1 skein embroidery floss to match the pink fleece
Thread to match fabric
Hand or machine sewing needle
Straight pins
Tapestry needle

Other Supplies

Pattern from the pattern sheet (scallop)
Rotary cutter
Ruler
Cutting mat
Water-soluble fabric marker
Scissors
Iron and pressing surface
Safety pin or elastic guide

Cutting Instructions

FROM THE PINK FLEECE, CUT:
Size infants (1) 9½" x 17" rectangle
Size small (1) 10" x 19" rectangle
Size medium (1) 11" x 20" rectangle
Size large (1) 12" x 24" rectangle

FROM THE ELASTIC, CUT:
Size infants (1) 15½" piece
Size small (1) 17" piece
Size medium (1) 18½" piece
Size large (1) 20" piece

Directions

This project uses a ⅝" seam allowance.

1. Make a plastic template: Use a pencil to trace the scallop pattern onto the clear plastic template sheet. Cut out the scallop template.

2. Place the fabric right-side up on a flat work surface. Place the scallop template on top of the fabric. Line up the scalloped edge of the template with the bottom edge of the skirt. Trace around the scallop pattern with a water-soluble fabric marker. Repeat, working your way from one end of the fabric to the other. Cut along the marked line.

3. Use six strands of pink floss and the tapestry needle to blanket stitch along the scalloped edge. See page 107 for a blanket stitch illustration.

4. With right sides together, stitch the short sides of the skirt, forming a tube.

5. Finish the top edge of the skirt using a serger, or fold under ¼" and stitch in place.

6. Turn the skirt inside out and place on a flat pressing surface. Fold the top opening of the skirt down 1½" and press. Be sure to use a setting compatible with fleece. Stitch all the way around the top of the skirt, 1¼" from the folded edge.

7. Attach an elastic guide or safety pin to one end of the elastic strip. Guide the elastic through the waistband. Overlap the edges, and stitch securely in place, using several rows of stitching. Adjust the fabric around the waistband and check the fit. Complete the stitching, stretching the elastic as needed, as you work. ➤

8. Fold up the scalloped hem of the skirt ½" and stitch in place along the scallops.

Pink Hat

The one thing I learned during the writing of this book, is that babies' head sizes can vary widely! If the baby you are making this hat for is available, measure his or her head, and add 1" to this measurement. Use this as the longer of the hat measurements and proceed as directed. If the baby is not available, use the sizes listed in the cutting instructions. Ally is 3 and wears a size large hat.

Fabrics (for all sizes)
¼ yd. pale pink fleece
6" square white fleece
6" square green fleece
4" square blue fleece

Notions
1 skein pink embroidery floss
Thread to match the fabric
Straight pins
Hand or machine sewing needle

Other Supplies
Rotary cutter
Ruler
Cutting mat
Water-soluble fabric marker
Scissors
Iron and pressing surface
Clear plastic template sheet
Pencil

Cutting Instructions
FROM THE PINK FLEECE, CUT:

Hat
Size infants (1) 7" x 16" rectangle
Size small (1) 7" x 17" rectangle
Size medium (1) 7½" x 18½" rectangle
Size large (1) 8" x 20" rectangle

Pompom
All sizes (1) 4" x 18" rectangle

Directions
This project uses a ⅝" seam allowance.

1. Use scissors to cut the pompom rectangle every ½". Cut ½" fringe along each long side, leaving the center uncut.

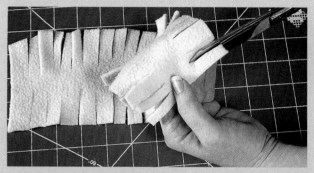

2. Pull each fringe strip, stretching it out and releasing it. The fringe will curl as you pull it. Gather along the center of the strip and pull tight. Tie with pink floss to secure.

3. Make a plastic template: Use a pencil to trace the scallop pattern onto the clear plastic template sheet. Cut out the scallop template.

4. Place the hat fabric right-side up on a flat work surface. Place the scallop template on top of the fabric. Line up the scalloped edge of the template with the bottom hem edge of the hat. Trace around the scallop pattern with a water-soluble fabric marker. Repeat, working your way from one end of the fabric to the other. Cut along the marked line.

5. Use six strands of pink floss and the tapestry needle to blanket stitch along the scalloped edge. See page 107 for a blanket stitch illustration.

6. With right sides together, stitch the short sides of the hat into a tube.

7. Turn the hat inside out. Gather along the top opening (the side without the scallop) and pull tight. Take several stitches to secure.

8. Make the flower: Gather around the edge of a white yo-yo circle, and pull tight, forming a pouch. Flatten and press. Repeat for the remaining white and blue yo-yos.

9. Gather across the straight edge of a green leaf and pull tight. Tie to secure. Repeat for the remaining leaf.

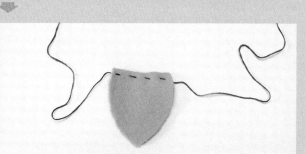

10. Turn the hat to the right side and stitch the pompom in place on the top of the hat.

11. Fold the scalloped edge of the hat up 2" and press. Be sure to use a setting compatible with fleece. Securely hand stitch two leaves in place on the hat front. Top with a white yo-yo, then a blue yo-yo. Securely stitch in place through all the layers. See page 11 for important safety instructions for adding appliqués to children's clothing.

Reversible Jacket

This jacket is completely reversible; it's like getting two projects in one. I chose a blue floss for the blanket stitch, to match the blue fleece. The green floss is a great contrast to the blue fleece. If you prefer, use green floss instead of blue.

Fabrics
1 yd. bright blue fleece
1 yd. bright green fleece

Notions
1 skein embroidery floss to match the green fleece
2 skeins embroidery floss to match the blue fleece
Tapestry needle
Thread to match fleece
Straight pins
Hand or machine sewing needle

Other Supplies
Patterns from the pattern sheet (jacket front and back)
Rotary cutter
Ruler
Cutting mat
Water-soluble fabric marker
Scissors
Iron and pressing surface

Cutting Instructions

FROM THE BLUE FLEECE, CUT:
(2) Jacket fronts
(1) Jacket back
Jacket pockets
Size infants and small (2) 3" squares
Size medium and large (2) 4" squares

FROM THE GREEN FLEECE, CUT:
(2) Jacket fronts
(1) Jacket back
Jacket pockets
Size infants and small (2) 3" squares
Size medium and large (2) 4" squares

Directions

This project uses a ⅝" seam allowance.

1. With right sides together, stitch the blue jacket fronts to the backs at the shoulder seams. Stitch each side seam from the bottom of the jacket to the end of the sleeve. Press. Repeat, using the green fleece.

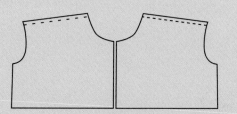

2. Blanket stitch across one edge of a blue pocket square using six strands of green floss and a tapestry needle. See page 107 for a blanket stitch illustration. Repeat for the remaining pocket square. Use six strands of blue floss and the tapestry needle to blanket stitch a blue pocket to each side of the green jacket front.

3. Blanket stitch across one edge of a green pocket square using six strands of blue floss and a tapestry needle. Repeat for the remaining pocket square. Use six strands of green floss and the tapestry needle to blanket stitch a green pocket to each side of the blue jacket front.

4. With wrong sides together, place the green jacket piece inside of the blue jacket piece. Pin in place along the bottom, neckline, sleeve openings and each side of the front.

5. Stitch the bottom, neckline, sleeve openings and each side of the front. Blanket stitch along each edge using the stitching line as a guide. Use six strands of blue floss and a tapestry needle.
To wear, turn the jacket to the side you like and turn up the cuffs to show the contrast lining.

Winter Blue Pants

I so wanted these pants to be reversible, but this fleece is just too fluffy and thick to make that feasible. (In some places, you would need to stitch though eight layers of fleece!) After breaking two needles on my machine, I gave up, and made these a single layer, with blanket-stitched cuffs for interest.

Fabrics (for all sizes)
⅝ yd. bright blue fleece
⅛ yd. bright green fleece

Notions
1 yd. ⅜" wide elastic
1 skein bright blue embroidery floss to
   match the fleece
Straight pins
Green sewing thread to match fleece
Hand or machine sewing needle

Other Supplies
Patterns from the pattern sheet
   (pants front and back, cuff)
Scissors
Iron and pressing surface
Safety pin or elastic guide

Cutting Instructions
FROM THE BLUE FLEECE, CUT:
(4) Pants (2 fronts and 2 backs)

FROM THE ELASTIC, CUT:
Size infants (2) 15½" lengths
Size small (2) 17" lengths
Size medium (2) 18½" lengths
Size large (2) 20" lengths

Directions
The project uses a ⅝" seam allowance.

1. With right sides together, stitch a
pants front to a back at side seams.
Stitch the front to the back at the inner
leg seams. Press. Repeat for the second
front and back.

2. With right sides together, insert one
pants leg inside of the other. Pin the
curved center seam and stitch. If you
are not using a serger, finish this seam as desired. Press.

3. Turn the pants inside out. Finish the top edge of the
pants using a serger, or fold under ¼" and stitch in
place.

4. Place the pants, inside out, on a flat pressing surface.
Fold the top edge of the pants down 1½" and press. Be
sure to use a machine setting compatible with fleece.
Stitch all the way around the top of the pants, ⅛" from
the folded edge.

5. Stitch around the top of the pants, ¾" from the
folded edge, leaving a 3" opening to insert the elastic.
Attach an elastic guide or safety pin to one edge of
the elastic. Guide the elastic through the waistband.
Overlap the edges, and stitch securely in place, using
several rows of stitching. Adjust the fabric around the
waistband and check the fit. Complete the stitching of
this row, stretching the elastic as needed as you work.

6. Stitch around the top of the pants, 1½" from the
folded edge, leaving a 3" opening to insert the elastic.
Attach an elastic guide or safety pin to one edge of
the elastic. Guide the elastic through the waistband.
Overlap the edges, and stitch securely in place, using
several rows of stitching. Adjust the fabric around
the waistband, then check the fit. Stitch the opening
closed.

7. Select one cuff piece. Place right sides together
and stitch along the short side. Press, forming a ring
of fabric. Fold the fabric ring in half with wrong sides
together and press. Stitch ⅜" from the folded edge.
Using the stitching as a guide, blanket stitch along
the folded edge using three strands of bright blue
embroidery
floss. See page
107 for a
blanket stitch
illustration.

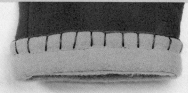

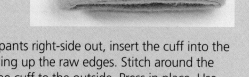

8. With the pants right-side out, insert the cuff into the
pants leg, lining up the raw edges. Stitch around the
edge. Turn the cuff to the outside. Press in place. Use
green thread to stitch through the cuffs at each side
seam to secure in place.

Blue Hat

Piecing the brim for this hat takes a bit of extra time, but I think the results are worth the effort! Fleece is a relatively expensive fabric, so I like to save my scraps for appliqué and accenting other pieces. If you don't have scraps handy, buy the smallest amount of fleece you can, usually one eighth of a yard.

Fabrics (for all sizes)

¼ yd. bright blue fleece
⅛ yd. light blue fleece
⅛ yd. green fleece

Notions

1 skein blue embroidery floss to match the fleece
Thread to match fleece
Hand or machine sewing needle
Straight pins

Other Supplies

Rotary cutter
Ruler
Cutting mat
Water-soluble fabric marker
Scissors
Iron and pressing surface

Cutting Instructions

FROM THE BRIGHT BLUE FLEECE, CUT:

Hat
Size infants (1) 7" x 16"
Size small (1) 7" x 17"
Size medium (1) 7½" x 18½"
Size large (1) 8" x 20"

Pompom
(1) 4" x 10" rectangle

Brim
Size infants (4) 2" x 6" rectangles
Size small and medium (5) 2" x 6" rectangles
Size large (6) 2" x 6" rectangles

FROM THE LIGHT BLUE FLEECE, CUT:
Brim
Size infants (4) 2" x 6" rectangles
Size small and medium (5) 2" x 6" rectangles
Size large (6) 2" x 6" rectangles

FROM THE GREEN FLEECE, CUT:

Pompom
(1) 4" x 10" rectangle

Brim
Size infants (4) 2" x 6" rectangles
Size small and medium (5) 2" x 6" rectangles
Size large (6) 2" x 6" rectangles

Note: *You may have rectangles left over when the hat is complete.*

Directions

This project uses a ⅝" seam allowance.

1. Use scissors to cut the pompom rectangles every ½". Cut ½" fringe along each long side, leaving the center uncut. Pull each fringe strip, stretching it out and releasing it. The fringe will curl as you pull it.

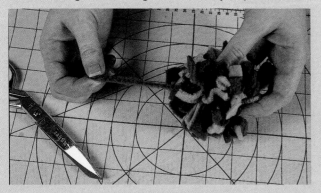

2. Gather along the center of the fringe strip and pull tight. Tie with blue floss to secure.

3. Piece the brim: Stitch the brim pieces, with right sides together along the 6" sides, alternating colors.
For infants: stitch 8 rectangles
For small: stitch 9 rectangles
For medium: stitch 10 rectangles
For large: stitch 11 rectangles

4. With right sides together, stitch the short sides of the hat piece forming a tube.

5. Turn the hat tube right-side out. Stitch the brim end pieces together, forming a ring. Fold the ring in half, with the seams facing in. Baste along the raw edges.

6. Place the brim ring inside the hat, match up the raw edges, and stitch in place.

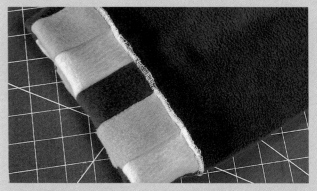

7. Fold the brim up into place, hiding the seam. Stitch in place at the back seam through all layers.

8. Turn the hat inside out, gather along the top opening (the side without the brim), and pull tight. Take several stitches to secure.

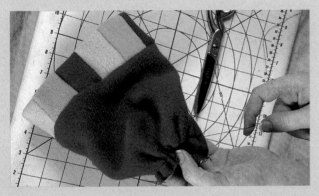

9. Turn the hat to the right side. Stitch the pompom in place on the top of the hat.

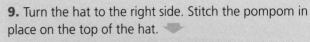

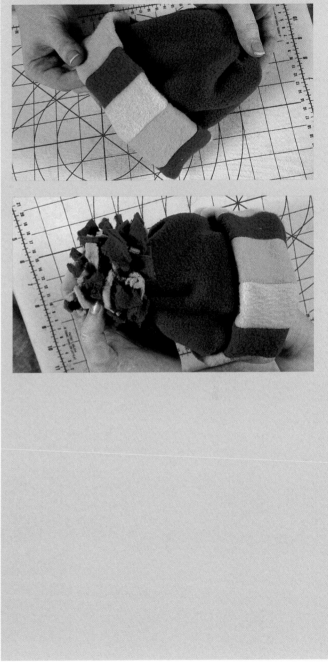

Chapter 7
Sewing and
Resource Guide

Cutting Out Patterns

There are two methods you can use to cut out pattern pieces:

1. Pin and cut: This is the traditional method. Pin the pattern piece in place on the fabric, with right sides of the fabric together and the print running in the right direction. Cut on the desired pattern line. Pattern weights can be used in place of pins, if desired.

2. Trace and cut: This is the method I use; it is a bit faster if you are making multiple garments, or intend to reuse the pattern. Trace the pattern onto a piece of poster board or plastic template. Label and cut out the template. To use, place the template piece on the fabric, with the right sides of the fabric together and the print running in the right direction. Use a fabric marker to trace around the edges of the template pattern piece, then cut on the traced line. Save the template pattern piece to reuse as needed.

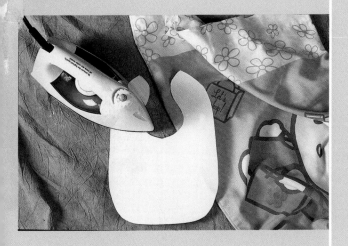

Pattern Sizes

The patterns included in this book range from infants to toddlers sizes. If your child is currently wearing a small size, you should trace the pattern you want to use onto a plastic template sheet, or onto freezer paper. This step allows you to preserve the larger sizes as your child grows.

Preserving Your Patterns

Tissue patterns tend to get a little worn out after you have used them a few times. To prolong the life of your patterns, iron each piece to the shiny side of freezer paper, then cut out. The paper will act as a stabilizer and your patterns will last much longer.

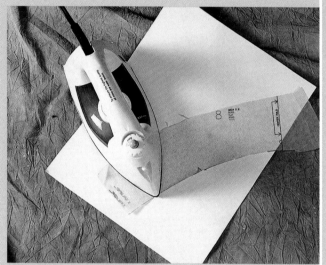

Freezer paper pattern

Making Yo-Yo Flowers

Yo-yos are very simple to make and provide a cute embellishment to any outfit. Follow the simple directions below to make a yo-yo.

1. Mark and cut a circle. The larger your circle is, the larger the finished yo-yo will be. Use the pattern provided on the pattern sheet, or trace around a small plate or saucer.

2. Hand gather around the edge of the circle.

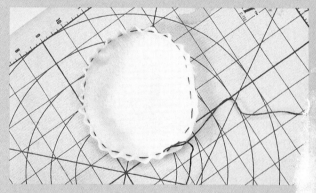

Gather the yo-yo

3. Pull the gathering strings, forming a pouch. Tie a knot to secure. Flatten and press.

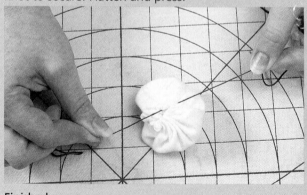

Finished yo-yo

Making Fabric-Covered Buttons

Even the tiniest scraps can be used for projects. Make buttons using project fabrics, or use tiny scraps of interesting patterns or embroidery. Finished buttons must be sewn on securely using proper safety precautions. The buttons shown here were made using scraps of a vintage handkerchief.

Fabrics

1" scraps of your desired fabrics

Other Supplies

¾" and 1½" buttons
(Cover Buttons kit by Prym-Dritz® were used for the samples. Kit includes all tools needed to make covered buttons.)
Scissors
Water-soluble fabric marker
Iron and pressing surface

Directions

For any sized button

1. Select a fabric scrap and place it right-side up on your pressing surface. Iron the scrap to remove any wrinkles.

2. Place the rounded disk portion of the button on top of the scrap. Using the water-soluble marker, mark a circle around the button. Mark a line ½" from the edge of the button. Your circle doesn't have to be perfect; the edges will not show in the finished product.

3. Use scissors to cut the fabric on the marked line.

4. Place the fabric, wrong side up, over the button maker.

Position the fabric

5. Use the rounded disk portion of the button to push the fabric into the button maker. The rounded portion of the button will snap into place. Tuck the fabric edges over the back of the button.

Cover the button

6. Place the button back, with the shank-side up, into the button maker. Use the pusher to snap the button into place.

Finish the button

Sewing Techniques

When stitching a project, you have three options: sew by hand, use a traditional sewing machine, or use a serger. Each has distinct advantages, and many times, I will combine all three techniques to complete a single garment.

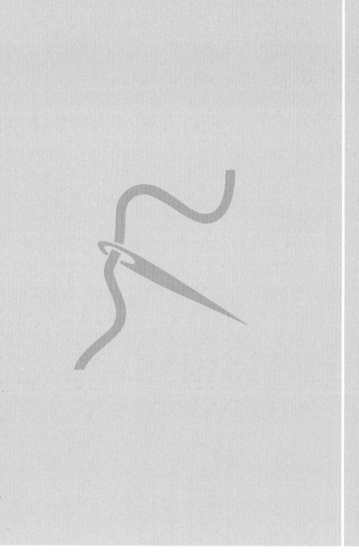

Sewing by hand

I will often grab a needle and hand stitch a portion of a garment or embellishment. I prefer to hand stitch yo-yos, shank buttons, appliqués, small areas of gathering and easing, hems and small areas I feel would be too difficult to reach by machine. Thread a hand sewing needle, tie a knot in the end of your thread, and start stitching. I save small hand stitching projects for long car or plane trips and keep a sewing basket on hand in the family room for those times when I have "just a minute" to sew.

I prefer to stitch appliqués by hand — it takes a little bit longer, but I like the finished look so much better. Stitch while you watch a movie or television; you will be amazed at how much you can complete during one program!

Sewing by traditional machine

A traditional sewing machine is one with a straight and a zigzag stitch. You do not need a fancy or expensive machine to sew children's clothing. The projects in this book were completed using a serger, and my very basic, 15-year-old Singer® sewing machine. Use a traditional sewing machine for securing stitching of seams and hems, for buttons and buttonholes, for gathering skirts and ruffles and for topstitching. If you choose not to use a serger, you can use a traditional machine to zigzag stitch over the raw seam edges of your garment for a more finished look.

topstitching on these pants was completed g a traditional sewing machine.

Sewing using a serger

A serger is a sewing machine that stitches and finishes seams in one step. Use a serger to add a professional look to any garment and to cut your sewing time substantially. My serger is a huge timesaver for straight seams and for finishing edges. I do prefer to use a traditional machine for sewing curved seams, as the serger cutting blade can sometimes take too big of a "bite" from an inwardly curved seam, resulting in a hole in the finished garment.

Pay special attention to the positioning of your fabric when you work on a serger. If you accidentally catch a portion of a garment in a seam using a traditional sewing machine, you can simply remove the seam and try again. If you catch a portion of a garment in a seam using a serger, you will ruin the garment.

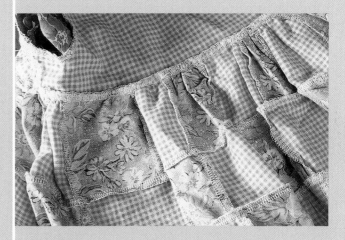

The skirt of this dress was pieced using a serger — finishing all those seams would have taken forever using a traditional machine!

Use your favorite methods to complete the projects in this book. For help with specific techniques, check out one of the many wonderful beginners' sewing guides available in any fabric store or bookstore.

Product Resource Information

Fabrics

Most of the fabrics in this book were purchased at quilting and fabric stores. Vintage linens used for projects can be found at a variety of locations, including antique shops, yard and garage sales, auctions and online.

Gem-Tac Glue™

Beacon Adhesives™
Mt. Vernon, NY 10550
(914) 699-3400
http://www.beaconcreates.com

Covered Button Kits

Prym-Dritz® Corporation
P. O. Box 5028
Spartanburg, SC 29304
(800) 255-7736
http://www.dritz.com

Basting Spray

Aerosol basting spray is a wonderful product. It can be used to baste quilts of all sizes, and to hold appliqué pieces in place as you work. Always use basting spray in a well-ventilated area, away from birds and other small pets. You will find a variety of basting sprays at your local quilt store.

Photography

Bobby Dalto, owner of Photographics Photography Studio, took the photos in this book.

3930 Wesley St. Suite 1205
Myrtle Beach, SC 29579
(843) 236-0982
The outdoor photos were shot on location at Huntington Beach State Park in Pawleys Island, S.C.